The Open
University

A103

AN INTRODUCTION TO
THE HUMANITIES

Resource Book 4

The Open University
Walton Hall, Milton Keynes
MK7 6AA

First published 1998

Edited, designed and typeset by The Open University.

Printed and bound by Scotprint Ltd., Musselburgh, Scotland.

ISBN 0 7492 8713 6

This text forms part of an Open University course A103 *An Introduction to the Humanities*. Details of this and other Open University courses can be obtained from the Course Reservations Centre, PO Box 724, The Open University, Milton Keynes MK7 6ZS; United Kingdom: telephone (00 44) 1908 653231.

For availability of this or other course components, contact Open University Worldwide Ltd, The Berrill Building, Walton Hall, Milton Keynes MK7 6AA, United Kingdom: tel. (00 44) 1908 858585, fax (00 44) 1908 858787, e-mail ouwenq@open.ac.uk

Alternatively, much useful course information can be obtained from the Open University's website http://www.open.ac.uk

a103rb4i1.1

Contents

Section A WRITING HISTORY

A1 Chronology of social, cultural and political events, 1954–75

Year	United Kingdom	North America	Continental Europe (West)	World
1954	Novel, *Lucky Jim*, by Kingsley Amis. Last of food rationing abolished.	In Brown v. Board of Education of Topeka US Supreme Court declares segregation in public schools illegal. Allen Ginsberg, Beat poet, settles in San Francisco.	Germany: Karlheinz Stockhausen, *Study II* (electronic music)	French routed in Indo-China (Vietnam). Revolt in Algeria.
1955	Conservatives (under Eden) re-elected. Mary Quant establishes Chelsea boutique *Bazaar*. English translation of Samuel Beckett play *Waiting for Godot*. Commercial television begins broadcasting.	Film, *Blackboard Jungle*, featuring Bill Hayley's 'Rock Around the Clock'. Chuck Berry has first success with 'Maybellene'. Little Richard song 'Tutti Frutti'. Nicholas Ray film *Rebel Without a Cause*, starring James Dean. Herbert Marcuse book *Eros and Civilization*. Emergence of Beat generation. Rosa Parks refuses to give up her seat to a white man on a segregated Montgomery, Alabama, bus. Martin Luther King leads a boycott of Montgomery buses.		

1956	Play, Look Back in Anger, by John Osborne. Suez crisis (Britain forced by American pressure to end operation against Egypt). London exhibition: Modern Art in the United States. British Pop art exhibition This is Tomorrow.	Film Rock Around the Clock. Elvis Presley becomes a national figure in music (Hound Dog, Heartbreak Hotel) and film.		Khrushchev denounces Stalin. Russia violently suppresses Hungarian independence movement.
1957	Prime Minister Harold Macmillan says 'some of our people have never had it so good'. Novel, Room at the Top, by John Braine. John Stephen established in Carnaby Street. Tour of Bill Hayley and his Comets.	Jack Kerouac's Beat novel, On the Road. President Eisenhower sends US army to Little Rock to enforce desegregation of central high school. Civil Rights Act – aimed (unsuccessfully) at safeguarding voting rights of blacks. Eugene Gilbert, Advertising and Marketing to Young People. Launch of TV programme American Bandstand. Leonard Bernstein musical, West Side Story.	Treaty of Rome sets up EEC. France: Political crisis over Algeria. International Situationists founded. West Germany: Equality of the Sexes Law.	Russians put first sputnik into space.

1958	CND (Campaign for Nuclear Disarmament) founded. Emergence of The Shadows, Cliff Richard, Lonnie Donnegan and Tommy Steele.	J.K. Galbraith book, *The Affluent Society* – criticizes 'public squalor' amidst corporate affluence. Mark Rothko, *The Seagram Murals* (1958–9).	France: May, De Gaulle to power. December, new constitution approved with De Gaulle as President with strong powers. Beginning of 'New Wave' in French cinema (Truffaut, Goddard, etc.). Claude Lévi-Strauss, *Anthropologie Structurale* – first statement of structuralist position. Italy: election of Pope John XXIII. Beginning of 'economic miracle'. Ministry of Health established.
1959	Film, *Room at the Top*. New 'permissive' Obscene Publications Act. William Glock becomes BBC Controller of Music. Race riots Nottingham and Notting Hill, London. Conservatives under Macmillan win third successive election victory. M. Abrams survey, *The Teenage Consumer*. Colin MacInnes novel about teenagers, *Absolute Beginners*. Mental Health Act.	Living Theatre achieves notoriety with Jack Gelber's play *The Connection*. Alan Kaprow's Happenings in Six Parts, New York. Miles Davis, *Kind of Blue*.	Italy: films, *La Dolce Vita* (Fellini) and *L'Aventura* (Antonioni). West Germany: Gunter Grass novel, *The Tin Drum*. France: Radio programme for young people, *Salut les copains*, established.

1960			
'Lady Chatterley Trial' makes possible publication of *Lady Chatterley's Lover*. Sir Hugh Greene Director-General of BBC. Film, *Saturday Night and Sunday Morning*. Harold Pinter plays, *The Birthday Party* and *The Caretaker*. Mary Quant goes wholesale, and visits America. The Beatles are the top group in Liverpool (but scarcely known elsewhere). Betting and Gaming Act (sets up betting shops). Immigration from Asia and West Indies accelerates. End of National Service. *Musica Reservata*, first public concert.	US Circuit Court of Appeals, New York, rules *Lady Chatterley's Lover* not obscene. US approves first birth-control pill Enovid safe for use. Black student 'sit-ins' against segregation begin in Greensboro, North Carolina, then spread throughout southern cities. Civil Rights Act, again aimed at voting rights. First televised presidential campaign debate between Kennedy and Nixon. Kennedy narrowly wins election. Student socialist organization SDS founded (Students for a Democratic Society). John Updike, *Rabbit Run* (sexually explicit novel). John Coltrane assembled his own band. Ornette Coleman, *Free Jazz*.	France: Yves St Laurent fashion house established. De Gaulle government institutes policy of subsidized local theatres throughout the country. *Nouveau Réealiste* group of artists formed in Paris. J.P. Sartre, *Critique de la raison dialectique* (reasserting traditional Marxism and *individualism* in repudiation of structuralism). Italy: Cassa per il Mezzogiorno (Fund for the South) begins to invest in southern industry. Luciano Berio, *Cirles* (voile, harp and percussion).	American U2 spy plane shot down over Central Russia. East–West Summit Conference subsequently collapses at opening session.

| 1961 | *Young Contemporaries* Art Exhibition features David Hockney and other young Pop artists.
End of football maximum wage.
Michael Tippett, *King Priam* (opera). | J.F. Kennedy inaugurated as President.
Cafe la Mama (experimental theatre) founded.
Peace Corps created.
Freedom Riders set out to test desegregation in South.
John C. Whitcomb, Jr and Henry Morris, *The Genesis Flood* ('bible' of anti-Darwinian creationism). | France: First family planning clinic.
Rightwing OAS (Secret Army Organization) founded to keep Algeria French.
Christiane Rochefort, *The Little Children of the Century* (first-person narrative by an observant and self-confident working-class girl – feminist and quite sexually explicit). | Russian cosmonaut Yuri Gagarin orbits earth.
Failed CIA-sponsored attempt at invasion of Cuba at Bay of Pigs.
Kennedy and Khrushchev meet at summit conference in Vienna.
East Germany builds Berlin Wall.
Soviet Union begins nuclear testing in atmosphere after three-year moratorium.
Kennedy sends first 400 US combat troops to South Vietnam.
Poland: Witold Lutoslawski, *Jeux vénitiens* (orchestra). |

| 1962 | Immigration Act. *That Was the Week That Was*, BBC current affairs satire show. First Bond film with Sean Connery as Bond (*Dr No*). Beatles 'Love Me Do' released. Benjamin Britten, *War Requiem*. | Helen Gurley Brown's book *Sex and the Single Girl*. Rachel Carson, *The Silent Spring* (environmentalist). Bob Dylan song 'Blowin' in the Wind' adopted by Civil Rights Movement. Death of Marilyn Monroe. Michael Harrington's book *The Other America* (about poverty coexisting with affluence). Kennedy's Social Welfare Amendments. SDS hold first national convention at Port Huron, Michigan. James Meredith attempts to enrol at University of Mississippi – Kennedy sends troops. Black writer James Baldwin publishes 'Letter From a Region in my Mind' (later called *The Fire Next Time*) in *New Yorker* – about white repression of black people. Sidney Janis Gallery New York has international show *The New Realists*. Andy Warhol has first major one-man show. Museum of Modern Art holds Symposium on *Pop Art*. | France: February, police charge at anti-OAS demonstration results in death of nine demonstrators at Charonne Metro Station, Paris. Youth magazine *Salut les copains* founded. Malraux law to protect historic areas of towns. Italy: Umberto Eco, *Opera Aperta* argues that modernist art and literature is characterized by openness to several interpretations. | American John Glenn orbits the earth. US resumes atmospheric nuclear testing. Algerian independence. Telstar satellite broadcasts first live intercontinental TV transmission. Russian missiles identified in Cuba. Kennedy orders blockade until missiles are removed. Khrushchev gives way. Russia: Aleksandr Solzhenitsyn, first novel, *One Day in the Life of Ivan Denisovich* (trans.1963). 11,000 US military personnel and technicians now aiding South Vietnam. India: Ravi Shankar, music for the ballet *Chandalika*. |

| 1963 | Experimental Traverse Theatre, Edinburgh, opens. Beatles records, 'From Me to You', 'She Loves You' and 'I Want to Hold Your Hand' successively top of the hit parade. ITV presents youth pop/rock programme *Ready Steady Go*. Rolling Stones start appearing in Richmond. Robbins Report on Higher Education – envisages building of many new universities. End of old football transfer system. Lindsay Anderson's film *This Sporting Life*. | Betty Friedan's book *The Feminine Mystique*. Mary MacCarthy's sexually explicit novel, *The Group*. Open Theatre and Bread and Puppet Theatre founded. Andy Warhol, *Red Race Riot*. Major Civil Rights Voter-Registration drive begins in Mississippi. Martin Luther King leads campaign against segregation in Birmingham, Alabama; Sheriff Bull Connor sets police dogs on demonstrators. Governor Wallace of Alabama bars admission of black students to University of Alabama. Kennedy speaks on TV on civil rights issue. Civil rights worker Medgar Evers murdered in Mississippi. Civil rights march on Washington concludes with M.L. King speech 'I Have a Dream'. Four black girls die in church bombing in Birmingham, Alabama. Kennedy assassinated in Dallas, Texas. Lyndon B. Johnson takes office. | France: Beginning of intensive campaign to bring electricity and inside bathrooms to rural areas. New Immigration Law. De Gaulle vetoes British application to join EEC. Italy: Social Security benefits extended. December: first of series of Centre/Left coalitions (including Socialists) which lasted until August 1969. | Nuclear Test Ban Treaty signed by US, USSR and UK. |

| 1964 | New teenage magazines, *Jackie* and *Fabulous*. Habitat (design shop) founded. Easter: Mods and Rockers riot at Clacton. Cambridge: First International Exhibition of Concrete and Kinetic poetry. Labour win power with tiny majority. Minister for the Arts appointed. | President Johnson (January) declares 'unconditional war on poverty' and (May) calls for creation of 'The Great Society'. Civil Rights Act, Economic Opportunity Act, Food Stamp Act. Bob Dylan song 'The Times They are a-Changin''. 'Freedom Summer' – continuing voter registration drive. After being missing forty-four days civil rights workers Schwerner, Goodman and Chaney found dead in Philadelphia, Mississippi. Student Free Speech Movement at Berkeley, California, led by Mario Savio of SDS, involved in violent confrontations. Igor Stravinsky, *Elegy for J.F.K.* (baritone and three clarinets). Herbert Marcuse, *One Dimensional Man* – envisages very poor and oppressed as a revolutionary force to be led by student radicals. Marshall McLuhan, *Understanding Media* – puts view that 'the medium is the message'. | Italy: Youth Magazine *Ciao Amici* established. | US Congress passes Gulf of Tonkin resolution authorizing full US involvement in Vietnam. |

| 1965 | The Who song, 'My Generation' ('hope I die before I get old'). Rolling Stones, 'I Can't Get No) Satisfaction'. Bob Dylan tour. Beatles album, *Rubber Soul*. CND anti-Vietnam War march. Capital punishment suspended for five years. Government committed to comprehensive schools. *New Generation* 'sculpture' exhibition at Whitechapel Art Gallery, London. *International Poetry Incarnation*, Albert Hall – poetry readings of 'underground poetry'. While destructive 'redevelopment' and building of urban motorways continues, first pedestrianization schemes are developed. TV programme, *Up the Junction*. | Establishment of San Francisco Bay Conservation and Development Commission. Medicare and Medicaid Amendments. Black Muslim leader Malcolm X assassinated. Civil rights march from Selma to Montgomery, Alabama under National Guard protection. Bob Dylan enrages audience by playing an electric set at Newport Folk Festival. Riots in black ghetto of Watts, Los Angeles. Ken Kesey and the Merry Pranksters hold first 'acid test' open to the public, San Francisco. Leonard Bernstein, *Chichester Psalms*. | France: Georges Perec novel, *Les Choses (Things)*. Althusser combines structuralism and traditional Marxism in *Pour Marx* and *Lire 'le Capital'*. Italy: Milana Mileni's sexually explicit novel *A Girl Named Jules* banned. | President Johnson orders bombing raids on North Vietnam (January). Mao Zedong institutes Cultural Revolution in China. Christmas halt to Vietnam bombing. Greece: Iannis Xenakis, *Normos Alpha* (solo cello). |

1966			
Labour wins power with secure majority. Ministry of Social Security Act. Race Relations Act. Vietnam Solidarity Campaign and Radical Students Alliance founded. Underground paper, *International Times (IT)* founded. Underground clubs (drugs and such groups as Pink Floyd and T Rex). Twiggy, aged 16, 'the face of 1966'. BBC documentary *Cathy Come Home* (about homeless single mother). Beginning of TV series *Till Death Us Do Part*. Jean Rhys novel, *Wide Sargasso Sea*. Beatles album, *Revolver*.	San Francisco Trips Festival – first hippie conclave. High-society author Truman Capote holds New York 'Black and White Ball' for the rich, the beautiful and the 'counter-cultural' – one guest is Andy Warhol. Federal Transport Act (contains environmental protection clause). Andy Warhol's underground film *Chelsea Girls* at New York's 41st Street Theatre (a commercial cinema). Simon and Garfunkel song 'The Dangling Conversation'. Bob Dylan album, *Blonde on Blonde*.	Italy: League for the Institution of Divorce founded. Troubles in secondary schools. *Zanzara* (Milan school magazine) seized by police for publishing sex survey. Beginning of intensive campaign to bring electricity and inside bathrooms to parts of rural Italy. Ultra feminist organization DEMAU founded. France: Ministry of Social Affairs established. Troubles in secondary schools. Michel Foucault publishes 'structuralist' study of the development of knowledge, *Les Mots et les Choses*. Germany: 'The Grand Coalition' – Christian Democrats and Social Democrats.	February: Bombing of North Vietnam resumes. US bombing raids on Hanoi (North Vietnam capital) and Haiphong. October: 320,000 US troops in Vietnam, outnumbering those of their South Vietnamese allies. Estonia: Arvo Pärt, Symphony No. 2.

1967				
	Film *Blow-up*, directed by Antonioni. Abortion Act, Family Planning Act, Act legalizing homosexual acts between two consenting adults in private. Welsh language placed on a par with English in Wales. Jimi Hendrix, brought over from America by the bass player and the manager of the group The Animals, has first hit with 'Hey Joe'. Beatles album, *Sergeant Pepper's Lonely Hearts Club Band*. Rolling Stones arrested on drugs charges. *Times* protests. Quickly released. London Arts Lab founded. Underground paper, *Oz*. First demonstration at American Embassy Grosvenor Square (basically against Vietnam War). Students sit-in at London School of Economics. Richard Rodney Bennett, music for the film *Far from the Madding Crowd*. David Munrow forms the Early Music Consort of London. Musica Reservata make their South Bank début. The Kinks song, 'Waterloo Sunset'. Plowden Report on Primary Education. Early Music Revival well under way. BBC TV, *The Forsyte Saga*.	San Francisco, Human Be-in. Joseph Papp's New York Shakespeare Festival Public Theatre founded. Takes over Cafe la Mama production which later became *Hair*. Broadway premier of Barbara Garson's play *MacBird*. April: 100,00 attend anti-Vietnam War demonstration in New York. June-August: Outbreak of pop festivals and hippie communes, summarized as 'Summer of Love'. June: Monterey Pop Festival. July: Black riots in Newark and Detroit (69 dead). August: The Maharishi – spiritual guide to the Beatles on Moral Regeneration and Transcendental Meditation – arrives in Los Angeles. October: The (anti-Vietnam War) March on the Pentagon.	Germany: Karlheinz Stockhausen, *Hymnen* (for orchestra and electronic sounds 4 track tape). Student troubles begin in Berlin over visit of Shah of Iran – one student killed by police. Italy: Troubles in universities. France: Troubles at Nanterre campus, in suburbs of Paris.	September: 464,000 US troops in Vietnam; 13,000 have been killed. October: Che Guevara, who had given up his post in the Cuban government to wage war against oppressive regimes, killed by the Bolivian army. Guevara posters become world-wide emblems of the protest movements. Japan: Toru Takemitsui, *November Steps* (biwa, shakulhachi and orchestra).

1968	March: Second (violent) Grosvenor Square demonstration. October: Peaceful Grosvenor Square demonstration. Student activism at Essex, Hornsey, Hull, Birmingham. Civil rights demonstrations in Northern Ireland. Theatres Act (abolishes censorship of Lord Chamberlain). *Hair* presented in London. Stanley Kubrick's *2001: A Space Odyssey* (filmed at Shepperton Studios).	February: Outbreak of garbage workers' strike in Memphis. March: Kerner commission report on civil disorders, 'our nation is moving toward two societies – one white, one black – separate and unequal'. April: Martin Luther King shot dead in Memphis, violence breaks out across country. April: Student strike and sit-ins at Columbia University, New York. Fair Housing Act. *Hair* opens on Broadway. June: Andy Warhol shot and seriously wounded by Valerie Solanas, founder and sole member of SCUM (Society for Cutting Up Men). Robert Kennedy assassinated. Film *The Graduate* – music by Simon and Garfunkel. August: Democratic convention Chicago – brutal violence perpetrated by Mayor Daley's police forces. First appearance of 'Myth of the Vaginal Orgasm' by Anna Koedt. Richard Nixon elected President.	Germany: Confrontations between police and students. Karlheinz Stockhausen, *Stimmung* for voices. Italy: Confrontations between police and students. *Arte Povera* Exhibition in Genoa. Plan to protect historic centre of Rome (November). Luciano Berio, *Sinfonia* for eight voices and orchestra. France: 'The events' of May-June (student demonstrations and occupations, violent confrontations with police). June: Election – overwhelming win for De Gaulle. Strikes – strikers keep students at arms length.	January to February: Vietcong Tet offensive very successful against Americans/South Vietnamese. December: US spacecraft orbits moon. India: The Beatles visit Maharishi Yogi in Rishikesh.

1969			
Voting age and age of majority reduced to 18. Divorce Reform Act. First Open University staff start work. British troops sent to Northern Ireland. Rolling Stones Hyde Park Concert. Isle of Wight Pop Festival. The Who rock opera, *Tommy*. Peter Maxwell Davies, *Eight Songs for a Mad King*. Permanent abolition of capital punishment.	March: Philip Roth's novel about masturbation *Portnoy's Complaint* heads best seller list. April: Black students exit from occupied student union building at Cornell University, Ithaca, New York, carrying guns. May: Violent confrontation begins at Berkeley. August: Woodstock Pop Festival, NY. Jimi Hendrix, 'Star Spangled Banner'. Women's Strike Day demonstration. September: Chicago conspiracy trial opens. October: Four violent 'days of rage' in Chicago by Weathermen, a splinter group of SDS. Vietnam moratorium day. December: Disastrous concluding Rolling Stones concert of 1969 tour at Altramont Speedway, California – gun-wielding black man stabbed to death by Hell's Angels and three others die. Beginning of relaxation in strict southern liquor laws. Gay Liberation appears in San Francisco Bay area.	*When Attitudes Become Form* – conceptual art exhibition tours Europe, comes to London in August. France: April: De Gaulle holds referendum. Dissatisfied with result, resigns. June: Pompidou elected President. Italy: The 'hot autumn' of working-class action. Various small feminist movements formed. Germany: Social Democrat Government.	January: 542,000 US troops in Vietnam – the peak number. July: President Nixon announces first troop withdrawals from Vietnam. Neil Armstrong and Buzz Aldrin walk on moon's surface.

| 1970 | Germaine Greer's book, The Female Eunuch.
Matrimonial Property Act (safeguards womens rights).
Equal Pay Act (voluntary until 1975 then compulsory).
Chronic Sick and Disabled Persons Act.
Second Isle of Wight Festival.
International Times (IT) Trial.
Women's liberation Conference, Oxford.
Women's Liberation disrupt Miss World contest.
Conservatives return to power. | Sexual Politics by Kate Millett and The Dialectic of Sex: The Case for Feminist Revolution by Shulamith Firestone.
February: Seven of Chicago Eight acquitted of conspiracy, but five convicted of individual acts of incitement to riot.
Bank of America branch burned down by students in Santa Barbara, California.
March: House in Greenwich Village, New York demolished by explosion of Weathermen Bomb Factory.
April: Earth Day.
May: At Kent State University, National Guards kill four student demonstrators and wound nine.
Washington demonstration of 100,000 against US invasion of Cambodia.
Jackson Mississippi State College – two black students killed, nine wounded by police.
September: President's Commission on campus unrest identifies gap between youth culture and established society as threat to American stability.
Voting Rights Act, but US Supreme Court rules that 18-year-olds can only vote in Federal Elections.
Theodore Roszak, The Making of a Counter Culture: Reflections on the Technocratic Society and its Youthful Opposition. | Italy: Divorce legalized. Workers' Charter.
Beginning of ultra-violent 'years of the bullet'; violence by Red Brigades and fascists.
France: Movement for Women's Liberation demonstration of behalf of unknown soldiers' unknown wife.
Elle Magazine organizes women's 'Estates General' – invaded by radical feminists.
September: First manifestation of gay liberation movement.
Germany: Beginning of Bader-Meinhoff gang terrorism. | May: President Nixon admits troops are in Cambodia.
June: US ground troops withdrawn from Cambodia. |

1971	March: Sugar and Spice feminist demonstration in Trafalgar Square. Feminist National Conference, London. OZ trial. London Weekend Television, *Upstairs Downstairs*.	Congress decides 18-year-olds can vote in all elections. April: Washington 250,000 demonstrate against continuation of Vietnam War; several hundred Vietnam veterans throw away their medals.	Germany: 18-year-olds get the vote. France: April: 343 famous women declare that they have had abortions. Homosexual Front for Revolutionary Action formed. Italy: February: First National Conference of MLD (Women's Liberation Movement). Women's Revolt publishes *Female Sexuality and Abortion*.	USSR: Dmitri Shostakovich, Symphony No.15.
1972	30 January: 'Bloody Sunday' in Northern Ireland – 14 unarmed civilians shot dead by Parachute Regiment. Angry Brigade trial. Violence at Salteley Coke Depot, Birmingham. Sit-ins at LSE, Hull and Stirling Universities. Feminist Magazine *Spare Rib* founded. IRA bomb attack at Aldershot. David Bowie album, *The Rise and Fall of Ziggy Stardust and the Spiders from Mars*.	June: Black leader Angela Davis acquitted by all-white jury of murder, kidnap and criminal conspiracy. Pornographic film *Deep Throat* widely exhibited. Richard Nixon re-elected President in landslide victory. Steve Reich, *Clapping Music*.	France: Bobigny Abortion trial – all defendants in effect acquitted.	

1973	Pink Floyd album, *Dark Side of the Moon*. Christopher Hogwood founds the Academy of Ancient Music.	US Senate establishes Senate committee to investigate Watergate Affair.	Britain joins EEC.	January: Peace Agreement in Paris ending Vietnam War. March: Withdrawal of US troops from Vietnam. International oil crisis: doubling of price of petrol.
1974	Labour return to office, but dependent on Liberals. IRA mainland bombing campaign intensifies. Clash between Trotskyites and National Front at Red Lion Square, London – Kevin Gately killed.	Nixon resigns – replaced by Gerald Ford – given free pardon.	Italy: Referendum upholds divorce. 18-year-olds get the vote. France: 18-year-olds get the vote. Ombudsman established.	Beginning of world-wide economic recession.
1975	Equal Pay Legislation comes into effect. Thames Television play about famous gay eccentric *The Naked Civil Servant*. Referendum confirms British membership of EEC. Margaret Thatcher elected Leader of the Conservatives.		France: Abortion legalized. Divorce law made even more liberal. Italy: Family Law – promise of 1948 Constitution at last implemented: husbands and wives to be equal; also children's rights recognized.	

A2 Brief pieces of statistical and social survey information

Except where otherwise stated this material comes from published government statistics.

United Kingdom

Increase in earnings, 1955–69

Increase in working-class earnings (basically manual wage-earners)	130 per cent
Increase in middle-class earnings (basically white-collar, professional and managerial workers)	127 per cent

Personal disposable income and consumer expenditure at constant 1970 prices in pounds

	1951	1961	1971	1972	1973	1974
Personal disposable income	390	532	638	680	719	724
Consumer expenditure	385	486	578	611	638	637

Families owning TV sets

1961	75 per cent
1971	91 per cent

Women who declared sex to be very important in marriage

1951	51 per cent
1969	67 per cent

(from social surveys conducted by Geoffrey Gorer)

United States of America

Total population in poverty

1959	22.4 per cent
1972	12.5 per cent

Black male income as percentage of white

1959	59 per cent
1969	67 per cent

Percentage of white females in white-collar jobs

1960	59 per cent
1970	61 per cent

Percentage of black females in white-collar jobs

1960	17 per cent
1970	32 per cent

Number of divorces per thousand of the population

1950	2.6
1955	2.3
1960	2.2
1965	2.6
1970	3.5
1971	3.7
1972	4.0

France

Growth in disposable income (salaries after tax), 1959–73

	1959–63	1963–9	1969–73
Top executives	2.8 per cent	2.9 per cent	3.5 per cent
Middle management	4.7 per cent	2.7 per cent	2.7 per cent
White-collar workers	4.2 per cent	3.0 per cent	4.4 per cent
Workers	4.3 per cent	3.0 per cent	4.9 per cent

French women who declared their sex life more liberated than ever before

1971	92 per cent

(from a survey in the French magazine L'Express)

Italy

Annual average increase in real income, 1963–74

South	4.2 per cent
Centre/North	3.8 per cent
All Italy	4.0 per cent

Industrial investment per employed person (1000 lire at constant 1975 prices)

	1961	1971	1975
South	593	1636	1478
Centre–North	825	804	789

1969 survey of 528 mothers (aged in fifties and sixties) and 528 married daughters (aged in twenties and thirties)

Q: Is sex fundamental to a woman's life?

A: Of mothers, 168 said yes, compared with 478 daughters.

Q: What most reinforces marriage?

A: Out of a list of twelve items, daughters put 'sex' at the top and 'communication and talking' second. Mothers put 'communication and talking' third bottom, and sex bottom.

(from a survey conducted by sociologist Lieta Harrison)

A3 Jim Haynes, *Thanks For Coming!*

From J. Haynes (1984) *Thanks For Coming! An Autobiography*, London, Faber and Faber, p.171.

As co-founder of the Traverse club in Edinburgh (1963) and later of the Arts Lab in London, Jim Haynes was a leading figure in 'counter-cultural' activities and the 'underground'. This is an extract from his reminiscences of the Sixties, published in 1984, *Thanks for Coming! An Autobiography*

> What we were doing in the colourful clothes and long hair in the sixties was telling people that we were tolerant, we were all for having fun, we were all for experimentation, we were all for making it new and making it exciting – it was quite extraordinary.
>
> The end of the sixties came as a kind of incredible collapse, a collapse of hope, and of the innocence and naivety of the decade when everyone felt that we were changing the world, that we could change the world. Then maybe a few people began to realise that through the music, through long hair and colourful costumes, through our attitudes, hopes and fears, we weren't going to change the world. We could only maybe change ourselves a bit. And I think this resulted in a depression for some people and a rush of cynicism.

A4 Allan Bloom, *The Closing of the American Mind*

From A. Bloom (1988 edn) *The Closing of the American Mind: How Higher Education has Failed Democracy and Impoverished the Souls of Today's Students*, New York, Touchstone Books, pp.313–14, 322, first published 1987.

Professor Allan Bloom, a senior American academic when he wrote the book these extracts are taken from, was a Professor of Political Science at Cornell University, New York State, during the troubles of the Sixties, when he was totally opposed to student activism. He has remained an extreme conservative ever since, and published *The Closing of the*

American Mind: How Higher Education has Failed Democracy and Impoverished the Souls of Today's Students in 1987. The long title adequately describes the nature of the book.

> The American university in the sixties was experiencing the same dismantling of the structure of rational inquiry as had the German university in the thirties. No longer believing in their higher vocation, both gave way to a highly ideologized student populace. And the content of the ideology was the same – value commitment. The universities had abandoned all claim to study or inform about value – undermining the sense of the value of what is taught, while turning over the *decisions* about values to the folk, the *Zeitgeist* [spirit of the age], the relevant. Whether it be Nuremberg or Woodstock, the principle is the same. As Hegel was said to have died in Germany in 1933, Enlightenment in America came close to breathing its last during the sixties. The fact that the universities are no longer in convulsions does not mean they have regained their health. [...]

> The sixties were the period of dogmatic answers and trivial tracts. Not a single book of lasting importance was produced in or around the movement. It was all Norman O. Brown and Charles Reich. This was when the real compromises hit the universities, when opinions about everything from God to the movies became absolutely predictable. The evidence brought from popular culture to bolster the case for the sixties – that in the fifties Lana Turner played torchy, insincere adulteresses while in the sixties we got Jane Fonda as an authentic whore, that before the sixties we had Paul Anka and after we had the Rolling Stones – is of no importance. Even if this characterization were true, it would only go to prove that there is no relation between popular culture and high culture, and that the former is all that is now influential on our scene. [...]

> Even the figures most seminal for 'the movement', like Marcuse, Arendt and Mills, did what serious work they did prior to 1960.

A5 Maureen Nolan and Roma Singleton, 'Mini-Renaissance'

From Sara Maitland (ed.) (1988) *Very Heaven: Looking Back at the 1960s*, London, Virago, pp.20, 24, 25.

Extracts from 'Mini-Renaissance' a memoir by Maureen Nolan and Roma Singleton who were teenagers in Liverpool in the mid Sixties.

> Young people suddenly had an important voice; they were being listened to, followed even, and Liverpool youth was at the front of this heady cultural thrust. It didn't matter any more that my scouse accent was raw and unrefined, there were people all over the country envying and trying to imitate the guttural tones that singled me out as a Liverpudlian. [...]

> The success of companies like Biba, who started making clothes very cheaply in that short shift style made famous by Jean Shrimpton, gave those of us who could thread a needle or crochet the inspiration to produce our own; and even if things did not quite turn out the way they should have,

they could still be passed off as a trial fashion of sorts – so much was being welcomed as new that mistakes were probably the origins of many trendy modes. It was a good idea if crocheting a dress to get the more intricate and dense flower patterns over the boobs, particularly if one was going bra-less. The problem with this particular fashion as far as I could see was that there must have been many girls, myself included, for whom going bra-less went unnoticed. [...]

And did all that upheaval in living standards, in attitudes and fashion have a lasting effect on the lives of the adults who were teenagers in Liverpool in the sixties? I believe it did. It gave us tolerance for new ideas, and brought us a step nearer to equality of rights, removing many prejudices of sexual, racial and moral origin. It gave us the freedom to accept or reject things on their own merits and according to our own individual preferences. I believe that the sixties were a mini-renaissance in which the right of individual expression was encouraged, applauded and nurtured by a generation whose naive belief was that all we needed was love.

A6 Report in the Los Angeles *Mirror News*

From *Mirror News*, Los Angeles, 29 October 1957

This is an extract from a report in the Los Angeles *Mirror News*, 29 October 1957. Elvis Presley had only become a national figure during 1956.

Sexhibitionist Elvis Presley has come at last in person to a visibly palpitating, adolescent female Los Angeles to give all the little girls' libidos the jolt of their lives.

Six thousand kids, predominantly feminine by a ratio of ten to one, jammed the Pan Pacific Auditorium to the rafters last night. They screamed their lungs out without let up as Elvis shook, bumped and did the grinds from one end of the stage to the other until he was a quivering heap on the floor thirty-five minutes later.

With anyone else the police would have closed the show ten minutes after it started. But not Elvis, our new national teenage hero.

A7 Report in the London *Evening Standard*

From *Evening Standard*, London, 31 October 1961

This is an extract from a London *Evening Standard* report on 31 October 1961 headlined '"Teenage Morals" and the Corruption of the Times'.

Miss Jo Drury said in her presidential address to the Association of Remand Home Superintendents and Matrons at Bournemouth today:

'Girls we are now getting have no sense of responsibility. They do not know right from wrong and there is only one subject they can talk about, and that is sex. They think that is part of their lives.'

Mr. Justice Stable, said at Lincs Assizes, Lincoln, today:

'It is an accepted thing today that these young people seem to attach as much importance to the act of sexual intercourse as they do to ordering an iced lolly.'

A8 Professor G.M. Carstairs, BBC Reith Lecture, 1962

From G.M. Carstairs (ed.) (1963) *This Island Now*, London, The Hogarth Press, pp.50–1.

The Reith lectures were and are a highly prestigious series of lectures given on BBC radio by some eminent authority. In 1962, under the series title *This Island Now*, they were given by G.M.Carstairs, Professor of Psychological Medicine at Edinburgh University. This extract is from the third lecture, 'Vicissitudes of Adolescence'.

> I believe that we may be mistaken in our alarm – at times amounting almost to panic – over young people's sexual experimentation. Contraception is still regarded as something wicked, threatening to chastity, opening the way to unbridled licence. But *is* chastity the supreme moral virtue? In our religious traditions the essence of morality has sometimes appeared to consist of sexual restraint. But this was not emphasised in Christ's own teaching. For him, the cardinal virtue was *charity*, that is consideration of and concern for other people. [...] It seems to me that our young people are rapidly turning our own society into one in which sexual experience, with precautions against conception, is becoming accepted as a sensible preliminary to marriage; a preliminary which makes it more likely that marriage, when it comes, will be a mutually considerate, a mutually satisfying partnership.

A9 Martin Luther King Jr, Letter from Birmingham Jail, 14 April 1963

From M.L. King Jr (1964) *Why We Can't Wait*, New York, New American Library, pp.74–5.

There follows an extract from a letter written by Martin Luther King from Birmingham Jail dated 14 April 1963. King was arrested for leading non-violent direct action against segregation in Birmingham, Alabama, widely recognized as the city in which segregation was most viciously enforced. The letter was written on the borders of newspapers and then, when these ran out, on toilet paper, and smuggled out of the prison. Polished up a bit by King himself, after his release from jail, it was then widely circulated as a pamphlet. We don't, of course, have the original hand-written version. The letter provides a good account of what was happening in Birmingham, Alabama, and of King's relationships with white ministers of religion, whom he is criticizing for describing his direct action as unwise and untimely.

> I think I should indicate why I am here in Birmingham, since you have been influenced by the view which argues against 'outsiders coming in' [...] I, along with several members of my staff, am here because I was invited here. [...]
>
> But more basically, I am in Birmingham because injustice is here. [...]
>
> You deplore the demonstrations taking place in Birmingham. But your statement I am sorry to say, fails to express a similar concern for the conditions that brought about the demonstrations. I am sure that none of you would want to rest content with the superficial kind of social analysis that deals merely with effects and does not grapple with underlying causes. It is unfortunate that demonstrations are taking place in Birmingham, but it is even more unfortunate that the city's white power structure left the Negro community with no alternative. [...]
>
> Birmingham is probably the most thoroughly segregated city in the United States. [...] There have been more unsolved bombings of Negro homes and churches in Birmingham than in any other city in the nation. These are the hard, brutal facts of the case. On the basis of these conditions, Negro leaders sought to negotiate with the city fathers. But the latter consistently refused to engage in good-faith negotiation.
>
> Then, last September, came the opportunity to talk with the leaders of Birmingham's economic community. In the course of the negotiations, certain promises were made by the merchants – for example, to remove the stores' humiliating racial signs. On the basis of these promises, the Reverend Fred Shuttleworth and the leaders of the Alabama Christian Movement for Human Rights agreed to a moratorium on all demonstrations. As the weeks and months went by, we realised that we were the victims of a broken promise. A few signs, briefly removed, returned; the others remained.
>
> As in so many past experiences, our hope had been blasted, and the shadow of deep disappointment settled upon us. We had no alternative except to prepare for direct action, whereby we would present our very bodies as a means of laying our case before the conscience of the local and national community. [...]
>
> You may well ask: 'Why direct action? Long sit-ins, marches and so forth? Isn't negotiation a better path?' You are quite right in calling for negotiation. Indeed, this is the very purpose of direct action. Non-violent direct action seeks to create such a crisis and foster such a tension that a community which has constantly refused to negotiate is forced to confront the issue.

A10 Betty Friedan, *The Feminine Mystique*

From B. Friedan (1963) *The Feminine Mystique*, London, Gollancz, pp.9, 377–8.

Married with young children, Friedan, during the four years or so prior to the publication of *The Feminine Mystique*, had become aware of the problem with no name, the discontent of married women faced with an image of femininity to which they did not really want to conform.

Gradually, without seeing it clearly for quite a while, I came to realise that something is very wrong with the way American women are trying to live their lives today. I sensed it first as a question mark in my own life, as a wife and mother of three small children, half guiltily and therefore half heartedly, almost in spite of myself, using abilities and education in work that took me away from home [...] There was a strange discrepancy between the reality of our lives as women and the image to which we were trying to conform, the image I came to call the feminine mystique. [...]

[W]hen women do not need to live through their husbands and children, men will not fear the love and strength of women, nor need another's weakness to prove their own masculinity. They can finally see each other as they are. And this may be the next step in human evolution.

Who knows what women can be when they are finally free to become themselves? Who knows what women's intellect will contribute when it can be nourished without denying love? Who knows of the possibilities of love where men and women share, not only children, home, and garden, not only the fulfilment of their biological roles, but the responsibilities and passions of the work that creates the human future and a full human knowledge of who they are. It has barely begun, the search of women for themselves. But the time is at hand when the voices of the feminine mystique can no longer drown out the inner voice that is driving women on to become complete.

A11 Letter from a young English academic, 3 January 1964

From a handwritten letter, the Bancroft Library, Berkeley, Henry Nash Smith Collection, Box 6, Folder 8.

This extract is from a letter written in October 1963 by a young English academic who has just returned to Cambridge after a period at the University of California at Berkeley. The letter is addressed to his senior colleagues at Berkeley.

For health and sanity these last months I've been going to twist and shake clubs which have sprung up all over London. We have a new group who may be visiting America soon, and here are worshipped as I think no other entertainer ever has been (I mean that – it's fantastic!). Called The Beatles – 4 kids from Liverpool, rough, cheeky, swingy, very much war-time kids, and full of gutsy energy. I must say I fell for their stuff when I got back. I never thought I'd live to twist and shake – but I have and I do [...] It is a relief to lose oneself in the unconscious hypnotic euphoria of the music.

A12 Open letter by academics at Berkeley, December 1964

From a letter in the Free Speech Movement Archives in the Bancroft Library, Berkeley, Box 2, Folder 7.

Though there had been violent student activism in Paris in 1963, the Berkeley 'Free Speech Movement' of 1964, strongly influenced by the Socialist SDS, is usually seen as the first coherent student movement. The police acted violently and provoked further violence. This open letter expresses the views of certain Berkeley academics.

As long as the 'Free Speech Movement' involved only a small portion of the Berkeley students, it was possible – all the more in the light of their actions – for many to regard them simply as a vociferous and sometimes disorderly minority.

But when among the 800 who were arrested on December 3 and the thousands who supported them we found a large proportion of our most mature and thoughtful students, we were impelled to take a more penetrating look at the reasons for their commitment. The young people are part of a generation which is quite different from those who, as educators, we have faced in the recent past. Many find themselves alienated from what they regard as a bureaucratised society, and from the increasingly impersonal University through which they have their major contact with that society. They are trying to find meaning for their lives, and finding it often outside the university in a commitment to the active social movements of today. To an unfortunate extent we, their faculties have lost touch with them. [...]

A13 Michael Schofield, *The Sexual Behaviour of Young People*

From M. Schofield, *The Sexual Behaviour of Young People*, London, Longman, 1965, p.29.

Extract from a pioneering survey, *The Sexual Behaviour of Young People*, organized in 1964 by Michael Schofield, Research Director of the Central Council for Health Education, and published in book form in 1965.

In the group of 478 younger boys (aged 15 to 17) a total of 55 (11%) said they had experienced sexual intercourse at least once. A total of 138 (30%) of the 456 older boys (aged 17 to 19) reported at least one experience of sexual intercourse. The figures for the girls are much smaller. Out of 475 younger girls, 29 (6%) said they had experienced sexual intercourse at least once. Among the older girls 73 (16%) out of the 464 reported at least one experience of sexual intercourse. Thus 20% of all the boys in the sample had experienced sexual intercourse and 12% of all the girls.

A14 Timothy Leary, Interview in *Playboy*, September 1966

From *Playboy*, September 1966, later published in G.P. Putnam (ed.) (1968) *The Politics of Ecstacy*, New York, Putnam, p.117.

This is an extract from an interview with Timothy Leary in the September 1966 edition of *Playboy*. Leary had a PhD in Clinical Psychology and in 1958 formed the Harvard Center for Research in Personality. In August 1960 he had 'the deepest religious experience of my life' after eating seven 'sacred mushrooms'. In 1963 he left Harvard and, with Richard Alpert, set up the privately funded international Foundation for Internal Freedom. He was *the* publicist for drugs as an indispensable aid to human progress. He also supported radical political causes and was several times arrested. The interview was later published in a collection of his writings.

> There *is* an LSD drop-out problem, but it's nothing to worry about. It's something to cheer. The lesson I have learned from over 300 LSD sessions, and which I have been passing on to others, can be stated in six syllables: turn on, tune in, drop out. 'Turn on' means to contact the ancient energies and wisdoms that are built into your nervous system. They provide unspeakable pleasure and revelation. 'Tune in' means to harness and communicate these new perspectives in a harmonious dance with the external world. 'Drop out' means to detach yourself from the tribal game. Current models of social adjustment – mechanized, computerized, socialized, intellectualized, televised, sanforized – make no sense to the new LSD generation, who see clearly that American society is becoming an air-conditioned anthill. In every generation of human history, thoughtful men have turned on and dropped out of the tribal game and thus stimulated the larger society can lurch ahead. Every historical advance has resulted from the stern pressure of visionary men who have declared their independence from the game: 'Sorry, George III, we don't buy your model! we're going to try something new'; 'Sorry, Louis XVI, we've got a new idea. Deal us out'; Sorry, LBJ, it's time to mosey on *beyond* the Great Society.

A15 Statement by LeRoi Jones, *Washington Free Press*, 4 August 1967

From Thomas Powers (1973) *The War at Home: Vietnam and the American People, 1964–1967*, New York, Grossman, p.218.

This is black writer, poet, and militant community organizer, LeRoi Jones, giving a press interview about the Newark riots, as reported in the black newspaper the *Washington Free Press*, 4 August 1967. In the Newark riots, which broke out on 13 July 1967, 26 people were killed, 1200 injured, and 1300 arrested. This extract is quoted in Thomas Powers, *The War at Home: Vietnam and the American People, 1964–1967*.

We had citizens of Newark, New Jersey, declare at this point that the unrest among black citizens cannot be characterised as a 'riot' or as a 'criminal action' on the part of black citizens. [...]

We understand that this unrest was a retaliation against the forces of oppression, brutality and legalised evil that exist within the city of Newark and that we citizens have the right to rebel against an oppressive, illiterate governmental structure that does not even represent our will. We will rule Newark or no one will! We will govern ourselves or no one will!

A16 Hubert G. Locke, *The Detroit Riot of 1967*

From H.G. Locke (1969) *The Detroit Riot of 1967*, Detroit, Wayne State University Press, pp.41, 43–5.

Locke was administrative assistant to Detroit Police Commissioner Ray Garadini at the time of the riot. This account was written up after the event using police and other eye-witness accounts, in addition to Locke's own observations. The riot began in the early hours of the morning of Sunday 23 July after a police raid on a packed 'blind pig' – an illegal drinking club patronized by black people. In his account Locke always makes it clear when citizens he refers to are white: the victims in this extract were black. Subsequent investigations revealed that in fact there were no snipers – only inexperienced National Guardsmen and police shooting at each other.

By midnight on the second day of the riot veteran police officers were convinced they were engaged in the worst encounter in urban guerrilla warfare ever witnessed in the United States in the 20th century. [...]

The fourth day, Wednesday

The early hours of Wednesday, July 26, turned out to be one of the worst periods of the riot. Of the 43 deaths occasioned by the riot, seven were the result of incidents that took place during the first three hours of Wednesday morning. Each of these incidents revealed tragic aspects of the riot; one became the most horrifying experience of the entire week. [...]

Four years old at the time of her death, Tanya Blanding was huddled in the living room of a second floor apartment [...] in the heart of the original riot area. [...] Sporadic sniper fire had been reported in the immediate area earlier in the evening and on the previous night. Guardsmen reported one of their units coming under fire [...] and believed they had pinpointed it as coming from the apartment in which Tanya and her family lived. Precisely what happened next is unclear; apparently as a guard tank was being moved into position directly in front of the building, one of the occupants of the building apartment lit a cigarette. Guardsmen opened fire with rifles and the tank's .50-calibre machine gun. At 1.20 am Tanya Blanding was dead.

There are as many versions concerning the death of 19-year-old William Dalton as there are persons to tell the story. The police log shows that shortly after midnight, specifically at 12.21 and 12.23, reports were broadcast that someone was breaking into a large moving and storage company warehouse. [...] Ten minutes later the warehouse was reported on fire and five minutes afterward the log carries a notation of sniper fire at the same location. What happened next depends on which story or witness one chooses to believe. According to one version, the police and guardsmen who arrived on the scene captured, ordered him to run, and then shot him as he fled. A second version recounts that as police arrived on the scene several youths, including Dalton, began to run in several directions, that the police ordered Dalton to halt and did not fire till he continued to flee. Dalton's body was found lying in the street [...] at 2.20 am.

A17   Letter written by the daughter of a rich Memphis family to her parents, 12 September 1967

From Van Dyke papers, Box 2, folder 226, Mississippi Valley Collection, Memphis State University.

Extract from a letter dated 12 September 1969 from the daughter (in her thirties) of a rich Memphis family to her parents, written from her home in Arkansas and after a visit to Los Angeles.

> We saw the teeny-boppers in their mini-skirts and fishnet stockings in Los Angeles; but I didn't believe the conservative Middle West would be caught dead in such gear. I must be wrong [...] [she went round the main shops in Arkansas] there wasn't a single dress I even wanted to try on. Everything is made for the junior figure [...] cut too short. Even my favourite Peck and Peck has deserted me for the mini-mod.

A18   UNEF statement, 'The truth about events of 10–11 May'

From Alain Schnapp and Pierre Vidal-Naquet (1969) *Journal de la Commune étudiante: textes et documents Novembre 1967–Juin 1968*, Paris, Editions de Seine, pp.224–5, translated by Arthur Marwick.

National Union of French Students (UNEF) statement issued 11 May 1968 entitled 'The Truth about the Events of 10–11 May' – a night of horrific violence by the Special Police Forces (CRS) against students, bystanders, and even local citizens inside their own flats in the Left Bank Latin Quarter or University area of Paris.

> For a week students have been struggling against police repression at the University.
> Before entering into any dialogue, the U.N.E.F. have insisted on three prior points:

A halt to the judicial and administrative procedures against demonstrators who have been imprisoned and their immediate release;

Withdrawal from the University quarter by all police forces;

The reopening of the University.

In the course of two previous demonstrations (Tuesday and Wednesday) the U.N.E.F. clearly showed that it had no wish to renew the violent confrontations with the police.

The day before yesterday again the orders issued by the U.N.E.F. were unambiguous: we do not wish to be responsible for any violence and demonstrators must abstain from any provocation towards the police. They should occupy the Latin Quarter, forming discussion groups while preparing themselves for eventual defence against attack by the considerable strength of the police forces massing around the Sorbonne.

THIS ADVICE WAS OBEYED

For nearly four hours, the students occupied the Latin quarter, perfectly peacefully, awaiting a public response from the government.

They got their response.

At a quarter past two in the morning, the police brutally attacked the demonstrators deploying not only simple tear gas grenades, but also chlorine and ammonia grenades, incendiaries and stun grenades.

The brutality of the repression was such that numerous people were wounded. At that time it was difficult to be sure of exact numbers.

After clearing a street, the C.R.S. painstakingly raided every house in order to drag out demonstrators who had taken refuge in them.

Many injured demonstrators were beaten up in police vehicles.

Nothing was done to facilitate the work of the ambulance services; in fact the police deliberately obstructed them.

Never has savagery reached such a paroxysm:

WHO IS RESPONSIBLE? WHO ISSUED THE ORDERS?

Faced with police repression, the students did not give way.

Faced with [missing in original] and grenades, they reaffirmed their [missing in original] with greater and greater determination as they realised that they were less and less isolated.

They ask the people, the workers, to give their support,

Students, and workers,

JOIN THE GENERAL STRIKE AND DEMONSTRATION ON MONDAY [...]

A19 Feliks Gross, *Il Paese: Values and Social Change in an Italian Village*

From F. Gross (1973) *Il Paese: Values and Social Change in an Italian Village*, with a preface by Vittorio Castellano, New York Universal Press, pp.128–9 and 137.

Extract from a survey conducted by American sociologist Feliks Gross in 1969 in a small community 60 kilometres south of Rome.

(a) Question-and-answer sessions with a local farmer.

Q. Is it better now than 12 years ago?

A. *Now it is better, much better. Everything has changed.*

Q. Do you eat better?

A. *Today a different style; yes, more like gentlemen. More meat, once, twice, three times a week.*

Q. And electricity?

A. *Now we have electricity. We are working now on conducting water to our houses [...] All the comforts. We move towards the better.*

Q. And refrigerators?

A. *Oh yes, people have refrigerators, radio, television [...]*

Q. The change is for the better?

A. *Very much so.*

(b) Report provided by a Roman professorial colleague, Professor G.N. Del Monte.

During another trip, a friend who is also a peasant, showed me his toilet; leading the way, he said with pride: 'We have a toilet, the Roman type [...]' It was plastered with tiles. I asked him: 'you remember not so long ago – we used to go in the middle of the field – not to a toilet. How do you feel today, when you go to the toilet?' Said he: 'I feel like a human being, like the others, not like an animal, as I felt before.'

A20 Evan Broadman, *Social Guide to New York Bars*

From E. Broadman (1969) *Social Guide to New York Bars*, New York, Collier Books, pp.40–41.

Broadman's is a special sort of 'guide book' aimed at New Yorkers as well as visitors to the city.

The majority of watering holes on the Upper East side, from 60th to 86th streets, on First, Second, and Third avenues, have evening specials for women on week days and brunches for everybody on Sundays. The evening specials starting at the cocktail hour (5:00) usually consists of drinks at half-price or free. And the reason is obvious. Gals attract the men. And the men are the spenders.

Almost every owner of a singles watering hole, alluded to the hesitancy of women to walk into a bar or saloon-restaurant alone. The Victorian stigma attached to a woman sitting at a bar persists. Liberation, it seems, does have it boundaries. But this is more than a vestige of an old-fashioned idea. No one wants to admit to loneliness, especially men. But the man has the advantage of being in his element at the bar; the woman sitting at the bar becomes fair game for a night in the sack.

Most of the women over 30 that we have talked to either firmly state, 'I don't sit at bars (alone)', or 'I just haven't got the courage to be put on display.' It makes a lot of sense. Having the odd-balls making pitches, snide remarks, and taking your being there as an invitation to bed, is pretty hard to stomach. *But times are changing and so is thinking.* Bars, saloons, and bar-restaurants in the better neighborhoods are perfectly acceptable meeting places. Instead of staying home nights, steeping in self-pity and bemoaning the scarcity of eligible men, more women [...] are going out to local watering holes [...]

Sunday afternoon in New York can serve the cautious girl as an easy-to-take introduction to the watering holes on the Upper East Side.

A21 Kate Millett, *Sexual Politics*

From K. Millett (1977 edn) *Sexual Politics*, New York, Virago, pp.25, 29, 362, 363, first published 1970.

At the time of publication Kate Millett was a young American academic, and leading figure in the new feminist movement. *Sexual Politics* was an immediate best-seller.

What goes largely unexamined, often even unacknowledged (yet is institutionalized none the less) in our social order, is the birthright priority whereby males rule females. Through this system a most ingenious form of 'interior colonization' has been achieved. It is one which tends moreover to be sturdier than any form of segregation, and more rigorous than class stratification, more uniform, certainly more enduring. However muted its present appearance may be, sexual dominion obtains nevertheless as perhaps the most pervasive ideology of our culture and provides its most fundamental concept of power.

This is so because our society, like all other historical civilizations, is a patriarchy. [...]

Not only is there insufficient evidence for the thesis that the present social distinctions of patriarchy (status, role, temperament) are physical in origin, but we are hardly in a position to assess the existing differentiations, since distinctions which we know to be culturally induced at present so outweigh them. Whatever the 'real' differences between the sexes may be, we are not likely to know them until the sexes are treated differently, that is alike. And this is very far from being the case at present. Important new research not only suggests that the possibilities of innate temperamental differences seem more remote than ever, but even raise questions as to the validity and permanence of psycho-sexual identity. In doing so it gives fairly concrete positive evidence of the overwhelmingly *cultural* character of gender, i.e. personality structure in terms of sexual category. [...]

Other progressive forces have recently asserted themselves, notably the revolt of youth against the masculine tradition of war and virility. Of course the most pertinent recent development is the emergence of a new feminist movement. Here again, it is difficult to explain just why such a development occurred when it did. [...]

When one surveys the spontaneous mass movements taking place all over the world, one is led to hope that human understanding itself has grown right for change. In America one may expect the new women's movement to ally itself on an equal basis with blacks and students in a growing radical coalition. It is also possible that women now represent a very crucial element capable of swinging the national mood, poised at this moment between the alternatives of progress or political repression, toward meaningful change. As the largest alienated element in our society, and because of their numbers, passion, and length of oppression its largest revolutionary base, women might come to play a leadership part in social revolution, quite unknown before in history. [...]

A22 Theodore Roszak, Preface to *The Making of a Counter Culture*

From T. Roszak (1970 edn) *The Making of a Counter Culture: Reflections on the Technocratic Society and Its Youthful Opposition*, London, Faber & Faber, Preface, pp.xi–xiii, first published 1969.

Roszak was (at the time) a young American academic. Most of the book had appeared previously as separate articles in the intellectual (though not scholarly) weekly *The Nation*, mainly about such Sixties figures as Marcuse, Leary and the beat poet Allen Ginsberg.

Thus the book itself reads more like a collection of disparate literary essays than as the coherent study promised in the Preface, which does, however, offer a perfect example of Roszak's literary style ('colleagues in the academy' is a long-winded way of saying 'academic colleagues'). The book was very successful, many of its purchasers clearly seeing themselves as part of this single 'counter culture'.

> As a subject of study, the counter culture with which this book deals possesses all the liabilities which a decent sense of intellectual caution would persuade one to avoid like the plague. I have colleagues in the academy who have come within an ace of convincing me that no such things as 'The Romantic Movement' or 'The Renaissance' ever existed – not if one gets down to scrutinizing the microscopic phenomena of history. At that level, one tends only to see many different people doing many different things and thinking many different thoughts. How much more vulnerable such broad-gauged categorizations become when they are meant to corral elements of the stormy contemporary scene and hold them steady for comment! And yet that elusive conception called 'the spirit of the times' continues to nag at the mind and demand recognition, since it seems to be the only way available in which one can make even provisional sense of the world one lives in. It would surely be convenient if these perversely ectoplasmic *Zeitgeists* were card-carrying movements, with a headquarters, an executive board, and a file of official manifestoes. But of course they

aren't. One is therefore forced to take hold of them with a certain trepidation, allowing exceptions to slip through the sieve of one's generalizations in great numbers, but hoping always that more that is solid and valuable will finally remain behind than filters away.

All this is by way of admitting openly that much of what is said here regarding our contemporary youth culture is subject to any number of qualifications. It strikes me as obvious beyond dispute that the interests of our college-age and adolescent young in the psychology of alienation, oriental mysticism, psychedelic drugs and communitarian experiments comprise a cultural constellation that radically diverges from values and assumptions that have been in the mainstream of our society at least since the Scientific Revolution of the seventeenth century. But I am quite aware that this constellation has much maturing to do before its priorities fall into place and before any well-developed social cohesion grows up around it.

At this point, the counter culture I speak of embraces only a strict minority of the young and a handful of their adult mentors. It excludes our more conservative young, for whom a bit less Social Security and a bit more of that old-time religion (plus more police on the beat) would be sufficient to make the Great Society a thing of beauty. It excludes our more liberal youth, for whom the alpha and omega of politics is no doubt still that Kennedy style. It excludes the scattering of old-line Marxist youth groups whose members, like their fathers before them, continue to tend the ashes of the proletarian revolution, watching for a spark to leap forth. More importantly, it excludes in large measure the militant black young, whose political project has become so narrowly defined in ethnic terms that, despite its urgency, it has become for the time being as culturally old-fashioned as the nationalist mythopoesis of the nineteenth century. In any event, the situation of black youth requires such special treatment as would run to book length in its own right.

If there is any justification for such exceptions in a discussion of youth, it must be that the counter cultural young are significant enough both in numbers and in critical force to merit independent attention. But from my own point of view, the counter culture, far more than merely 'meriting' attention, desperately requires it, since I am at a loss to know where, besides among these dissenting young people and their heirs of the next few generations, the radical discontent and innovation can be found that might transform this disoriented civilization of ours into something a human being can identify as home. They are the matrix in which an alternative, but still excessively fragile future is taking shape. Granted that alternative comes dressed in a garish motley, its costume borrowed from many and exotic sources – from depth psychiatry, from the mellowed remnants of left-wing ideology, from the oriental religions, from Romantic *Weltschmerz* [agony over the state of the world], from anarchist social theory, from Dada and American Indian lore, and, I suppose, the perennial wisdom. Still it looks to me like all we have to hold against the final consolidation of a technocratic totalitarianism in which we shall find ourselves ingeniously adapted to an existence wholly estranged from everything that has ever made the life of man an interesting adventure.

If the resistance of the counter culture fails, I think there will be nothing in store for us but what anti-utopians like Huxley and Orwell have forecast – though I have no doubt that these dismal despotisms will be far more stable and effective than their prophets have foreseen. [...]

A23 The Bobigny Abortion Trial, 1972

From *Association Choisir* (1973) *Avortement: Une loi en proces: L'Affaire de Bobigny*, 'Sterotypie integrale des débate au tribunal de Bobigny (8 Novembre 1972)', Paris, pp.55, 141–2, 270.

Extracts from the transcript of the 1972 trial at Bobigny (a working-class outer suburb of Paris) of Madame Chevalier (for procuring an abortion), Madame Bambuck (for carrying out the abortion), and Madames Duboucheix and Sausset (for acting as intermediaries). Chevalier, Duboucheix and Sausset all worked together on the Paris Metro. Madame Chevalier had expressed her willingness to help her daughter, Marie-Claire, to bring up her baby, but 16-year-old Marie-Claire had insisted on going ahead with the abortion. It turned out disastrously, and Marie-Claire's life was only saved by expensive medical treatment. A few weeks before, a juvenile court, held in private, had totally acquitted Marie-Claire (later, she explained how she derived great courage from the noisy feminist demonstration outside). The main defence was organized by the feminist pro-abortion organization, *Association Choisir* (*Choice*), and led by the distinguished Tunisian barrister, Gisèle Halimi. The three extracts printed here are taken (a) from the prosecution case, (b) from the testimony of Madame Sausset, who had herself been abandoned as a baby, and brought up under the horrors of Public Assistance, and (c) the final address to the presiding judges by Halimi. It should be noted that several of France's most distinguished male medical and academic experts testified for the defence. Although, as the prosecuting counsel announced, it was illegal to publish the proceedings of an abortion trial, a complete transcript was in fact published by *Association Choisir* (without any action being taken against them).

(a)   And so, is the law today really so bad as people say? I think that the proposition upon which it is founded lives on since it is based on respect for life, on the respect for one's self and the respect for other people. We must remember that all of us, wherever we are, rich or poor, educated or not, we have only merged from the state of being a foetus (laughter in court). We must quietly affirm, whether our birth was desired or not, that in general we are happy to have life. If our parents had been free to commission abortions, it is probable that a certain number among us, even among the most distinguished, would not now be in this world. [...]

As far as Mme Michelle Chevalier is concerned, she bears a heavy responsibility in this matter. She is the one who made the arrangements, who was actually present at the abortion, and she is the one who deliberately in full awareness gambled with the life of the one she calls her little daughter. She also has had her difficulties; I bear these in mind and recognize that apart from this case, she is an honourable woman. There are, of course, extenuating circumstances, but in her case I must demand a serious sentence.

As far as Mme Duboucheix and Mme Sausset are concerned, the matters of which they are accused stand somewhat apart from the actual crime, since they simply served as intermediaries, putting the abortionist in contact with Mme Chevalier. For them, I request a token sentence.

(b)   When Mme Chevalier asked me to help her, I had a choice: to be the accomplice to an abortion or the accomplice in abandoning a baby. For it was quite clear, and Marie-Claire had said it over and over again – that if she were obliged to have the baby, she would abandon it to the Public Assistance. And so, Monsieur Le President, I did not hesitate. Between being the accomplice to an abortion and the accomplice to abandoning a baby, I chose to be the accomplice to an abortion, and that is why I am here. [...]

c)   If there are still serfs in the world, they are women; she is a serf, since she is brought before you, Gentlemen, when she has disobeyed your law, when she aborts.

She is brought before you. Is that the most certain sign of our oppression? Excuse me, Gentlemen, but I have decided to say everything tonight. Look at yourselves and look at us [...] These four women in front of these four men! [...]

Would you be willing, Gentlemen, to be brought before a tribunal of women because of what you do with your own bodies? [...] That would seem crazy! (Loud applause) [...]

Gentlemen, it is your duty today to say that a new era begins in which the old world is abandoned. (Loud applause)

[Sentence was pronounced two weeks later. Duboucheix and Sausset were acquitted. Chevalier was sentenced to a fine of 500 francs, immediately suspended. Bambuck was sentenced to one year in prison, immediately suspended.]

Section B COUNTER-MOVEMENTS IN SCIENCE

B1 Theodore Roszak, 'The technocracy'

From T. Roszak (1969) *The Making of a Counter Culture: Reflections on the Technocratic Society and Its Youthful Opposition*, Garden City, N.Y., Doubleday, Anchor Books, Chapter 1, pp.5–9, 12–13.

By the technocracy, I mean that social form in which an industrial society reaches the peak of its organizational integration. It is the ideal men usually have in mind when they speak of modernizing, up-dating, rationalizing, planning. Drawing upon such unquestionable imperatives as the demand for efficiency, for social security, for large-scale co-ordination of men and resources, for ever higher levels of affluence and ever more impressive manifestations of collective human power, the technocracy works to knit together the anachronistic gaps and fissures of the industrial society. [...]

In the technocracy, nothing is any longer small or simple or readily apparent to the non-technical man. Instead, the scale and intricacy of all human activities – political, economic, cultural – transcends the competence of the amateurish citizen and inexorably demands the attention of specially trained experts. Further, around this central core of experts who deal with large-scale public necessities, there grows up a circle of subsidiary experts who, battening on the general social prestige of technical skill in the technocracy, assume authoritative influence over even the most seemingly personal aspects of life: sexual behavior, child-rearing, mental health, recreation, etc. In the technocracy everything aspires to become purely technical, the subject of professional attention. [...]

Within such a society, the citizen, confronted by bewildering bigness and complexity, finds it necessary to defer on all matters to those who know better. Indeed, it would be a violation of reason to do otherwise, since it is universally agreed that the prime goal of the society is to keep the productive apparatus turning over efficiently. In the absence of expertise, the great mechanism would surely bog down, leaving us in the midst of chaos and poverty. [...] [T]he roots of the technocracy reach deep into our cultural past and are ultimately entangled in the scientific world-view of the Western tradition. But for our purposes here it will be enough to define the technocracy as that society in which those who govern justify themselves by appeal to technical experts who, in turn, justify themselves by appeal to scientific forms of knowledge. And beyond the authority of science, there is no appeal.

Understood in these terms, as the mature product of technological progress and the scientific ethos, the technocracy easily eludes all traditional political categories. Indeed, it is characteristic of the technocracy to render itself ideologically invisible. Its assumptions about reality and its values become as unobtrusively pervasive as the air we breathe. While daily political argument continues within and between the capitalist and collectivist societies of the world, the technocracy increases and consolidates its power in both as a transpolitical phenomenon following the dictates of industrial efficiency, rationality, and necessity. In all these arguments, the technocracy assumes a position similar to that of the purely neutral umpire in an athletic contest. The umpire is normally the least obtrusive person on the scene. Why? Because we give our attention and passionate allegiance to the teams, who compete within the rules; we tend to ignore the man who stands above the contest and who simply interprets and enforces the rules. Yet, in a sense, the umpire is the most significant figure in the game, since he alone sets the limits and goals of the competition and judges the contenders.

The technocracy grows without resistance, even despite its most appalling failures and criminalities, primarily because its potential critics continue trying to cope with these breakdowns in terms of antiquated categories. This or that disaster is blamed by Republicans on Democrats (or vice versa), by Tories on Labourites (or vice versa), by French Communists on Gaullists (or vice versa), by socialists on capitalists (or vice versa), by Maoists on Revisionists (or vice versa). But left, right, and center, these are quarrels between technocrats or between factions who subscribe to technocratic values from first to last. The angry debates of conservative and liberal, radical and reactionary touch everything except the technocracy, because the technocracy is not generally perceived as a political phenomenon in our advanced industrial societies. It holds the place, rather, of a grand cultural imperative which is beyond question, beyond discussion.

When any system of politics devours the surrounding culture, we have totalitarianism, the attempt to bring the whole of life under authoritarian control. We are bitterly familiar with totalitarian politics in the form of brutal regimes which achieve their integration by bludgeon and bayonet. But in the case of the technocracy, totalitarianism is perfected because its techniques become progressively more subliminal. The distinctive feature of the regime of experts lies in the fact that, while possessing ample power to coerce, it prefers to charm conformity from us by exploiting our deep-seated commitment to the scientific world-view and by manipulating the securities and creature comforts of the industrial affluence which science has given us. [...]

[T]he prime strategy of the technocracy [...] is to level life down to a standard of so-called living that technical expertise can cope with – and then, on that false and exclusive basis, to claim an intimidating omnicompetence over us by its monopoly of the experts. Such is the politics of our mature industrial societies, our truly *modern* societies, where two centuries of aggressive secular skepticism, after ruthlessly eroding the traditionally transcendent ends of life, has concomitantly given us a proficiency of technical means that now oscillates absurdly between the production of frivolous abundance and the production of genocidal munitions.

B2   Theodore Roszak, 'A counter culture'

From T. Roszak (1969) *The Making of a Counter Culture: Reflections on the Technocratic Society and Its Youthful Opposition*, Garden City, N.Y., Doubleday, Anchor Books, Chapter 2, pp.42, 43–4, 47–9, 50–51.

What is special about the generational transition we are in is the scale on which it is taking place and the depth of antagonism it reveals. Indeed, it would hardly seem an exaggeration to call what we see arising among the young a 'counter culture'. Meaning: a culture so radically disaffiliated from the mainstream assumptions of our society that it scarcely looks to many as a culture at all, but takes on the alarming appearance of a barbaric intrusion. [...]

Toynbee has identified such cultural disjunctures as the work of a disinherited 'proletariat', using as his paradigm the role of the early Christians within the Roman Empire – a classic case of Apollo being subverted by the unruly centaurs. The Christian example is one that many of the hip young are quick to invoke, perhaps with more appropriateness than many of their critics may recognize. Hopelessly estranged by ethos and social class from the official culture, the primitive Christian community awkwardly fashioned of Judaism and the mystery cults a minority culture that could not but seem an absurdity to Greco-Roman orthodoxy. But the absurdity, far from being felt as a disgrace, became a banner of the community.

> For it is written [St. Paul boasted] I will destroy the wisdom of the wise, and will bring to nothing the understanding of the prudent. ... For the Jews require a sign, and the Greeks seek after wisdom. ... But God hath chosen the foolish things of the world to confound the wise; and God hath chosen the weak things of the world to confound the things which are mighty.
> (I Cor. 1:19, 22, 27)

It is a familiar passage from what is now an oppressively respectable source. So familiar and so respectable that we easily lose sight of how aggressively perverse a declaration it is ... how loaded with unabashed contempt for a long-established culture rich with achievement. And whose contempt was this? That of absolute nobodies, the very scum of the earth, whose own counter culture was, at this early stage, little more than a scattering of suggestive ideas, a few crude symbols, and a desperate longing. It was the longing that counted most, for not all the grandeur of Greco-Roman civilization could fill the desolation of spirit Christianity bred upon. [...]

Perhaps the young of this generation haven't the stamina to launch the epochal transformation they seek; but there should be no mistaking the fact that they want nothing less. 'Total rejection' is a phrase that comes readily to their lips, often before the mind provides even a blurred picture of the new culture that is to displace the old. [...]

For the orthodox culture they confront is fatally and contagiously diseased. The prime symptom of that disease is the shadow of thermonuclear annihilation beneath which we cower. The counter culture takes its stand against the background of this absolute evil, an evil which is not defined by the sheer *fact* of the bomb, but by the total *ethos* of the bomb, in which our politics, our public morality, our economic life, our intellectual endeavor are now embedded with a wealth of ingenious rationalization. We are a civilization sunk in an unshakeable commitment to genocide, gambling madly with the universal extermination of our species. And how viciously we ravish our sense of humanity to pretend, even for a day, that such horror can be accepted as 'normal', as 'necessary'! Whenever we feel inclined to qualify, to modify, to offer a cautious 'yes ... *but*' to the protests of the young, let us return to this fact as the decisive measure of the technocracy's essential criminality: the extent to which it insists, in the name of progress, in the name of reason, that the unthinkable become thinkable and the intolerable become tolerable.

If the counter culture is [...] that healthy instinct which refuses both at the personal and political level to practice such a cold-blooded rape of our human sensibilities, then it should be clear why the conflict between young and adult in our time reaches so peculiarly and painfully deep. In an historical emergency of absolutely unprecedented proportions, we are that strange, culture-bound animal whose biological drive for survival expresses itself *generationally*. It is the young, arriving with eyes that can see the obvious, who must remake the lethal culture of their elders, and who must remake it in desperate haste. [...]

And [...] how shall we characterize the counter culture they are in the way of haphazardly assembling? Clearly one cannot answer the question by producing a manifesto unanimously endorsed by the malcontented younger generation: the counter culture is scarcely so disciplined a movement. It is something in the nature of a medieval crusade: a variegated procession constantly in flux, acquiring and losing members all along the route of march. Often enough it finds its own identity in a nebulous symbol or song that seems to proclaim little more than 'we are special ... we are different ... we are outward-bound from the old corruptions of the world'. Some join the troop only for a brief while, long enough to enter an obvious and immediate struggle: a campus rebellion, an act of war-resistance, a demonstration against racial injustice. Some may do no more than flourish a tiny banner against the inhumanities of the technocracy; perhaps they pin on a button declaring 'I am a human being: do not mutilate, spindle, or tear.' Others, having cut themselves off hopelessly from social acceptance, have no option but to follow the road until they reach the Holy City. No piecemeal reforms or minor adjustments of what they leave behind would make turning back possible for them.

But where is this Holy City that lies beyond the technocracy – and what will it be like? Along the way, there is much talk about that, some of it foolish, some of it wise. Many in the procession may only be certain of what it must *not* be like. A discerning few [...] have a shrewd sense of where the technocracy leaves off and the New Jerusalem begins: not at the level of class, party, or institution, but rather at the non-intellective level of the personality from which these political and social forms issue. They see, and many who follow them find the vision attractive, that building the good society is not primarily a social, but a psychic task. What makes the youthful disaffiliation of our time a cultural phenomenon, rather than merely a political movement, is the fact that it strikes beyond ideology to the level of consciousness, seeking to transform our deepest sense of the self, the other, the environment. [...]

What is it that has allowed so many of our men of science, our scholars, our most sophisticated political leaders, even our boldest would-be revolutionaries to make their peace with the technocracy – or indeed to enter its service so cheerfully? Not lack of intellect or ignorance of humane values. It is rather that technocratic assumptions about the nature of man, society, and nature have warped their experience at the source, and so have become the buried premises from which intellect and ethical judgment proceed.

In order, then, to root out those distortive assumptions, nothing less is required than the subversion of the scientific world view, with its entrenched commitment to an egocentric and cerebral mode of consciousness. In its place, there must be a new culture in which the non-intellective capacities of the personality – those capacities that take fire from visionary splendor and the experience of human communion – become the arbiters of the good, the true, and the beautiful. I think the cultural disjuncture that generational dissent is opening out between itself and the technocracy is just this great, as great in its implications (though obviously not as yet in historical import) as the cleavage that once ran between Greco-Roman rationality and Christian mystery. To be sure, Western society has, over the past two centuries, incorporated a number of minorities whose antagonism toward the scientific world view has been irreconcilable, and who have held out against the easy assimilation to which the major religious congregations have yielded in their growing desire to seem progressive. Theosophists and fundamentalists, spiritualists and flat-earthers, occultists and satanists ... it is nothing new that there should exist anti-rationalist elements in our midst. What *is* new is that a radical rejection of science and technological values should appear so close to the center of our society, rather than on the negligible margins. It is the middle-class young who are conducting this politics of consciousness, and they are doing it boisterously, persistently, and aggressively – to the extent that they are invading the technocracy's citadels of academic learning and bidding fair to take them over.

B3 Theodore Roszak, 'The myth of objective consciousness'

From T. Roszak (1969) *The Making of a Counter Culture: Reflections on the Technocratic Society and Its Youthful Opposition*, Garden City, N.Y., Doubleday, Anchor Books, Chapter 7, pp.207, 208–15, 216–17, 229–30, 233, 234–6, footnotes omitted.

[I]f the technocracy is dependent on public deference to the experts, it must stand or fall by the reality of expertise. But what *is* expertise? What are the criteria which certify someone as an expert? [...]

An expert, we say, is one to whom we turn because he is in control of reliable knowledge about that which concerns us. In the case of the technocracy, the experts are those who govern us because they know (reliably) about all things relevant to our survival and happiness: human needs, social engineering, economic planning, international relations, invention, education, etc. Very well, but what is 'reliable knowledge'? How do we know it when we see it? The answer is: reliable knowledge is knowledge that is scientifically sound, since science is that to which modern man refers for the definitive explication of reality. And what in turn is it that characterizes scientific knowledge? The answer is: objectivity. Scientific knowledge is not just feeling or speculation or subjective ruminating. It is a verifiable description of reality that exists independent of any purely personal considerations. It is true ... real ... dependable. ... It works. And that at last is how we define an expert: he is one who *really* knows what is what, because he cultivates an objective consciousness.

Thus, if we probe the technocracy in search of the peculiar power it holds over us, we arrive at the myth of objective consciousness. There is but one way of gaining access to reality – so the myth holds – and this is to cultivate a state of consciousness cleansed of all subjective distortion, all personal involvement. What flows from this state of consciousness qualifies as knowledge, and nothing else does. This is the bedrock on which the natural sciences have built; and under their spell all fields of knowledge strive to become scientific. The study of man in his social, political, economic, psychological, historical aspects – all this, too, must become objective: rigorously, painstakingly objective. At every level of human experience, would-be scientists come forward to endorse the myth of objective consciousness, thus certifying themselves as experts. And because they know and we do not, we yield to their guidance.

* * *

But to speak of 'mythology' in connection with science would se first glance to be a contradiction in terms. Science, after all, purpo be precisely that enterprise of the mind which strips life of its myth substituting for fantasy and legend a relationship to reality based, in William James' phrase, on 'irreducible and stubborn facts'. [...] [W]ith the advent of the scientific world view, indisputable truth takes the place of make-believe.

There is no doubting the radical novelty of science in contrast to all earlier mythological world views. What all non-scientific cultural systems have had in common is the tendency to mistake their mythologies for literal statements about history and the natural world – or at least the tendency to articulate mythological insights in what a scientific mind mistakes for propositional assertions. In this way, imaginative expressions rich in moral drama or psychic perception easily degenerate into fabulous conjectures about the exotic reaches of time and space. This is how we most often use the word 'mythology' in our time: to designate the telling of unverifiable, if not downright false, tales about remote ages and places. The story of the Garden of Eden is a 'myth' we say, because insofar as any believing Christian or Jew has ever tried to locate the story geographically and historically, skeptics have been able to call his evidence, if any, quite cogently into question. [...]

[T]here is no way around the painful dilemma in which the religious traditions of the world have found themselves trapped over the last two centuries. Every culture that has invested its convictions in a temporal-physical mythology is doomed before the onslaught of the scientific unbeliever. Any village atheist who persists in saying 'show me' is in the position to hold up to ransom an entire religious culture, with little expectation that it will be able to find the price demanded. It would be difficult to say whether this situation partakes more of farce or of tragedy. Only a few generations ago, Clarence Darrow, no more than a skillful courtroom lawyer armed with a Sunday supplement knowledge of Darwin, was able to make laughingstock of a Judeo-Christian mythology that had served to inspire the finest philosophical and artistic minds of our culture over hundreds of generations. Yet, under unrelenting skeptical pressure, what choice have those who cling to temporal-physical mythologies but to undertake strategic retreat, conceding ever more ground to secular, reductionist styles of thought. [...]

Unlike the mythological traditions of the past, science is not in the first instance a body of supposed knowledge about entities and events. [...] What scientists know may [...] wax or wane, change in part or whole as time goes on and as evidence accumulates. If the Piltdown fossil proves to be a hoax, it can be discarded without calling the science of physical anthropology into question. If the telescopes of astronomers were to discover angels in outer space, science as a method of knowing would not be in any sense discredited; its theories would simply be reformulated in the light of new discoveries. In contrast to the way we use the phrase 'world view' in other contexts, science rests itself not in the *world* the scientist beholds at any particular point in time, but in his mode of *viewing* that world. A man is a scientist not because of what he sees, but because of *how* he sees it.

At least, this is what has become the conventional way of regarding scientific knowledge. Thomas Kuhn [...] has recently thrown strong and significant doubt on this 'incremental' conception of the history of science. His contention comes close to suggesting that the progressive accumulation of 'truth' in the scientific community is something of an illusion, created by the fact that each generation of scientists rewrites its textbooks in such a way as to select from the past what is still considered valid and to suppress the multitude of errors and false starts that are also a part of the history of science. As for the all-important principles of validation that control this natural selection of scientific truth from era to era – the so-called 'scientific method' – Kuhn is left unconvinced that they are quite as purely 'rational' or 'empirical' as scientists like to think.

Yet the incremental conception of scientific knowledge is very much part of the mythology we are concerned with here. The capacity of science to progress stands as one of the principal validations of its objectivity. Knowledge progresses only when it is understood to survive the passing of particular minds or generations. Science, understood as the expanding application of a fixed method of knowing to ever more areas of experience, makes such a claim. A scientist, asked to explain why science progresses when other fields of thought do not, would doubtlessly refer us to the 'objectivity' of his method of knowing. Objectivity, he would tell us, is what gives science its keen critical edge and its peculiarly cumulative character.

Are we using the word 'mythology' illegitimately in applying it to objectivity as a state of consciousness? I think not. For the myth at its deepest level is that collectively created thing which crystallizes the great, central values of a culture. It is, so to speak, the intercommunications system of culture. If the culture of science locates it highest values not in mystic symbol or ritual or epic tales of faraway lands and times, but in a mode of consciousness, why should we hesitate to call this a myth? The myth has, after all, been identified as a universal phenomenon of human society, a constitutive factor so critical in importance that it is difficult to imagine a culture having any coherence at all if it lacked the mythological bond. Yet, in our society, myth as it is conventionally understood has become practically a synonym for falsehood. To be sure, we commonly hear discussion of various social and political myths these days (the myth of the American frontier, the myth of the Founding Fathers, etc.); the more enlightened clergy even talk freely of 'the Christian myth'. But myths so openly recognized as myths are precisely those that have lost much of their power. It is the myth we accept without question as truth that holds real influence over us. [...]

Objectivity as a state of being fills the very air we breathe in a scientific culture; it grips us subliminally in all we say, feel, and do. The mentality of the ideal scientist becomes the very soul of the society. We seek to adapt our lives to the dictates of that mentality, or at the very least we respond to it acquiescently in the myriad images and pronouncements in which it manifests itself about us during every waking hour. The Barbarella and James Bond who keep their clinical cool while dealing out prodigious sex or sadistic violence ... the physiologist who persuades several score of couples to undertake coitus while wired to a powerhouse of electronic apparatus so that he can achieve a statistical measure of sexual normalcy [...] the Secretary of Defense who tells the public without blinking an eye that our country possesses the 'overkill' capacity to destroy any given enemy ten times [...] the celebrated surgeon who assures us that his heart transplant was a 'success' though of course the patient died ... the computer technician who blithely suggests that we have to wage an 'all-out war on sleep' in order to take advantage of the latest breakthrough in rapid communications [...] all these (or so I would argue) are life under the sway of objective consciousness. [...]

Consider the strange compulsion our biologists have to synthesize life in a test tube – and the seriousness with which this project is taken. Every dumb beast of the earth knows without thinking once about it how to create life: it does so by seeking delight where it shines most brightly. But, the biologist argues, once we have done it in a laboratory, *then* we shall really know what it is all about. Then we shall be able to *improve* upon it!

What a measure of our alienation it is that we do not regard that man as a fool who grimly devotes his life to devising routine laboratory procedures for that which is given to him like a magnificent gift in the immediacy of his own most natural desire. It is as if the organism could not be trusted with a single one of its natural functions, but this brain of ours must be brought forward to control and supervise and make sure everything is running along as efficiently as a well-programmed machine. [...]

Once conceive of human consciousness in this way, and the inevitable next step is to replace it with a machine just as good ... or better. So we come to the ultimate irony: the machine which is a creature of the human being becomes – most fully in the form of the computerized process – its maker's ideal. The machine achieves the perfect state of objective consciousness and, hence, becomes the standard by which all things are to be gauged. It embodies the myth of objective consciousness as Jesus incarnated the Christian conception of divinity. [...]

When [...] those of us who challenge the objective mode of consciousness are faced with the question 'but is there any *other* way in which we can know the world?', I believe it is a mistake to seek an answer on a narrowly epistemological basis. Too often we will then find ourselves struggling to discover some alternative method to produce the same sort of knowledge we now derive from science. There is little else the word 'knowledge' any longer means besides an accumulation of verifiable propositions. The only way we shall ever recapture the sort of knowledge Lao-tzu referred to in his dictum 'those who know do not speak', is by subordinating the question 'how shall we know?' to the more existentially vital question 'how shall we live?' [...]

When we challenge the finality of objective consciousness as a basis for culture, what is at issue is the size of man's life. We must insist that a culture which negates or subordinates or degrades visionary experience commits the sin of diminishing our existence. [...] It is not of supreme importance that a human being should be a good scientist, a good scholar, a good administrator, a good expert; it is not of supreme importance that he should be right, rational, knowledgeable, or even creatively productive of brilliantly finished objects as often as possible. Life is not what we are in our various professional capacities or in the practice of some special skill. What *is* of supreme importance is that each of us should become a person, a whole and integrated person in whom there is manifested a sense of the human variety genuinely experienced, a sense of having come to terms with a reality that is awesomely vast.

It is my own conviction that those who open themselves in this way and who allow what is Out-There to enter them and to shake them to their very foundations are not apt to finish by placing a particularly high value on scientific or technical progress. I believe they will finish by subordinating such pursuits to a distinctly marginal place in their lives, because they will realize that the objective mode of consciousness, useful as it is on occasion, cuts them off from too much that is valuable. They will therefore come to see the myth of objective consciousness as a poor mythology, one which diminishes life rather than expands it; and they will want to spend little of their time with it. That is only my hunch; I could be wrong.

But of this there can be no doubt: that in dealing with the reality our non-intellective powers grasp, *there are no experts*. The expansion of the personality is nothing that is achieved by special training, but by a naive openness to experience.

B4 Theodore Roszak, 'Objectivity unlimited'

From T. Roszak (1969) *The Making of a Counter Culture: Reflections on the Technocratic Society and Its Youthful Opposition*, Garden City, N.Y., Doubleday, Anchor Books, Appendix, pp.269, 275–89.

The items contained in this appendix are meant to give at least a minimal illustration of the psychology of objective consciousness [...] The examples offered are few in number; but they could be multiplied many times over. [...]

(1)   The first item dates back nearly a century; but it is cited without criticism in a recent survey of psychology as a significant example of pioneering neurological research. It concerns the work of Dr Roberts Bartholow of the Medical College of Ohio. In 1874 Dr Bartholow conducted a number of experiments on a 'rather feeble-minded' woman of thirty named Mary Rafferty. The experiments involved passing an electric current into the young woman's brain through a portion of the skull that had eroded away. Here is a selection from the records of Dr Bartholow, who introduces his findings by saying, 'It has seemed to me most desirable to present the facts as I observed them, without comment.'

> *Observation* 3. Passed an insulated needle into the left posterior lobe. ... Mary complained of a very strong and unpleasant feeling of tingling in both right extremities. In order to develop more decided reactions, the strength of the current was increased. ... her countenance exhibited great distress, and she began to cry. ... left hand was extended ... the arms agitated with clonic spasms, her eyes became fixed, with pupils widely dilated, lips were blue and she frothed at the mouth. (Quoted in David Krech, 'Cortical Localization of Function', in Leo Postman, ed., *Psychology in the Making* [New York: A.A. Knopf, 1962], pp.62–63.)

Three days after this experiment, Mary Rafferty was dead. Those who think such experimentation on human specimens – especially on imprisoned persons like Mary Rafferty – is uncommon, should see M.H. Pappworth's *Human Guinea Pigs: Experimentation on Man* (London: Routledge & Kegan Paul, 1967).

(2)   To spare a sigh for the fate of animals undergoing laboratory experimentation is generally considered cranky in the extreme. The reasons for this no doubt include the layman's inability to gain a clear picture of what is happening to the animals through the technical terminology of such accounts as appear in the many journals of physiology, psychology, and medical research, as well as the prevailing assumption that such research is directly related to human benefit and is therefore necessary. The following is a fairly comprehensive report of research done for the British Ministry of Supply during World War II on the effects of poison gases. If the account detours into too many technicalities, the situation is simply this: the experimenter has forced a large dose of Lewisite gas into the eye of a rabbit and is recording over the next two weeks precisely how the animal's eye rots away. But note how the terminology and the reportorial style distance us from the reality of the matter. As in the case of Mary Rafferty above, it is impossible to focus on the fact that the event is happening before a human observer.

> *Very severe lesions ending in loss of the eye:* ... In two eyes of the 12 in the series of very severe lesions the destructive action of the Lewisite produced necrosis [decay] of the cornea before the blood vessels had extended into it.

Both lesions were produced by a large droplet. In one case the rabbit was anaesthetized, in the other it was not anaesthetized and was allowed to close the eye at once, thus spreading the Lewisite all over the conjunctival sac [eyeball]. The sequence of events in this eye begins with instantaneous spasm of the lids followed by lacrimation in 20 seconds (at first clear tears and in one minute 20 seconds milky Harderian secretion). In six minutes the third lid is becoming oedematous [swollen] and in 10 minutes the lids themselves start to swell. The eye is kept closed with occasional blinks. In 20 minutes the oedema [swelling] is so great that the eye can hardly be kept closed as the lids are lifted off the globe. In three hours it is not possible to see the cornea and there are conjunctival petechiae [minute hemorrhages]. Lacrimation continues.

In 24 hours the oedema is beginning to subside and the eye is discharging muco-pus. There is a violent iritis [inflammation] and the cornea is oedematous all over in the superficial third. ... On the third day there is much discharge and the lids are still swollen. On the fourth day the lids are stuck together with discharge. There is severe iritis. The corneae are not very swollen. ... On the eighth day there is hypopyon [pus], the lids are brawny and contracting down on the globe so that the eye cannot be fully opened. ... In 10 days the cornea is still avascular, very opaque and covered with pus. On the 14th day the center of the cornea appears to liquify and melt away, leaving a Descemetocoele [a membrane over the cornea], which remains intact till the 28th day, when it ruptures leaving only the remains of an eye in a mass of pus. (Ida Mann, A. Pirie, B.D. Pullinger, 'An Experimental and Clinical Study of the Reaction of the Anterior Segment of the Eye to Chemical Injury, With Special Reference to Chemical Warfare Agents', *British Journal of Ophthalmology*, Monograph Supplement XIII, 1948, pp.146–47.)

By way of explaining the methodological validity of such research, P.B. Medawar offers the following hard-headed observation:

For all its crudities, Behaviorism, conceived as a methodology rather than as a psychological system, taught psychology with brutal emphasis that 'the dog is whining' and 'the dog is sad' are statements of altogether different empirical standing, and heaven help psychology if it ever again overlooks the distinction. (P.B. Medawar, *The Art of the Soluble* [London: Methuen, 1967], p.89.)

Professor Medawar does not make clear, however, on whom the 'brutal emphasis' of this distinction has fallen: the experimenter or the experimental subject. Does it, for example, make any difference to the methodology if the subject is capable of saying, 'I am sad', 'I am hurt'?

For a wise discussion of the ethics and psychology of animal experimentation (as well as a few more ghastly examples of the practice), see Catherine Roberts, 'Animals in Medical Research' in her *The Scientific Conscience* (New York: Braziller, 1967).

(3) The following comes from a study of the effects of war-time bombing on civilian society, with special reference to the probable results of thermonuclear bombardment. The research was done under grants from the US Air Force and the Office of the Surgeon General at the

Columbia University Bureau of Applied Social Research, and published with the aid of a Ford Foundation subsidy. It should be mentioned that the scholar's conclusions are generally optimistic about the possibilities of rapid recovery from a nuclear war. He even speculates that the widespread destruction of cultural artifacts in such a war might have the same long-term effect as the barbarian devastation of Greco-Roman art and architecture: namely, a liberation from the dead hand of the artistic past such as that which prepared the way for the Italian Renaissance.

> We have deliberately avoided arousing emotions. In this area, which so strongly evokes horror, fear, or hope, a scientist is seriously tempted to relax his standards of objectivity and to give vent to his own subjective feelings. No one can fail to be deeply aroused and disturbed by the facts of nuclear weapons. These sentiments are certainly necessary to motivate actions, but they should not distort an investigation of the truth or factual predictions.

> This book deals with the social consequences of actual bombing, starting with different types of destruction as given physical events, tracing step by step the effects upon urban populations – their size, composition, and activities – and finally investigating the repercussions upon national populations and whole countries. ... While we are deeply concerned with the moral and humanitarian implications of bomb destruction, we excluded them from this book, not because we judged them to be of secondary importance, but because they are better dealt with separately and in a different context.

This 'different context', however, has not to date been explored by the author. But he does turn to considering 'the effect upon morale' of wholesale carnage. Note how the use of phrases like 'apparently' and 'it appears' and 'it can be argued' and 'there is evidence of' neatly denature the horror of the matters under discussion.

> The impact of casualties upon morale stems mainly from actually seeing dead or injured persons and from the emotional shock resulting from the death of family and friends. ... No other aspect of an air raid causes as severe an emotional disturbance as the actual witnessing of death and agony. Interviews with persons who have experienced an atomic explosion reveal that 1/3 of them were emotionally upset because of the casualties they saw, while only 5 percent or fewer experienced fear or some other form of emotional disturbance on account of the flash of the explosion, the noise, the blast, the devastation, and the fires.

> An atomic bombing raid causes more emotional reactions than the conventional raid. Janis declares:

> 'Apparently it was not simply the large number of casualties but also the specific character of the injuries, particularly the grossly altered physical appearance of persons who suffered severe burns, that had a powerful effect upon those who witnessed them. Hence, it appears to be highly probable that, as a correlate of the exceptional casualty-inflicting properties of the atomic weapon, there was an unusually intense emotional impact among the uninjured evoked by the perception of those who were casualties.'

> The strong emotional disturbance that results from the sight of mangled bodies has also been reported from lesser peacetime disasters such as a plant explosion.
>
> We are interested here in this emotional agitation only as it affects the overt behavior of city dwellers. Two contradictory reactions could be suggested as short-range effects. It can be argued that apathy and disorganization will prevail. On the other hand, it is conceivable that the emotional disturbance from casualties will intensify rescue or defense activities. While there is evidence of both forms of reactions after a disaster, the latter is encouraged by effective leadership which directs survivors toward useful activities. (Fred C. Iklé, *The Social Impact of Bomb Destruction* [Norman, Okla.: University of Oklahoma Press, 1958], pp.vii–viii; 27–29.)

(4)   As the selection above suggests, the new social science of operations analysis has done an impressively ambitious job of opening up hitherto neglected avenues of research. Here, for example, are some suggested research subjects for which the RAND Corporation received government grants totaling several million dollars during 1958 as part of its civilian defense studies:

> A study should be made of the survival of populations in environments similar to overcrowded shelters (concentration camps, Russian and German use of crowded freight cars, troopships, crowded prisons, crowded lifeboats, submarines, etc.). Some useful guiding principles might be found and adapted to the shelter program.

The object of such research would be to 'act as reassurance that the more unpleasant parts of the experience had been foreseen and judged to be bearable by a peacetime government'. (Herman Kahn, 'Some Specific Suggestions for Achieving Early Non-Military Defense Capabilities and Initiating Long-Range Programs', RAND Corporation Research Memorandum RM-2206-RC, 1959, pp.47–48.)

And to give but one more example of the truly Faustian élan of our military-oriented research, we have this prognosis from a naval engineer:

> Weather and climate are never neutral. They are either formidable enemies or mighty allies. Try to imagine the fantastic possibilities of one nation possessing the capability to arrange over large areas, or perhaps the entire globe, the distribution of heat and cold, rain and sunshine, flood and drought, to the advantage of itself and its allies and to the detriment of its enemies. We *must* think about it – *now* – for this is the direction in which technology is leading us. ...
>
> The question is no longer: 'Will mankind be able to modify the weather on a large scale and control the climate?' Rather, the question is: 'Which scientists will do it first, American or Russian?' ... (Commander William J. Kotsch, USN, 'Weather Control and National Strategy', *United States Naval Institute Proceedings*, July 1960, p.76.)

(5)   The classic justification for technological progress has been that it steadily frees men from the burdens of existence and provides them with the leisure in which to make 'truly human uses' of their lives. The

following selections would suggest, however, that by the time we arrive at this high plateau of creative leisure, we may very well find it already thickly inhabited by an even more beneficent species of inventions which will have objectified creativity itself. It is quite unclear what the justification for this form of progress is, other than the technocratic imperative: 'What can be done must be done.'

> I would like to teach a machine how to write a limerick, and I suspect I can do it. I am quite sure that in the first batch it will be easy for anybody to pick out from a random array those limericks created by an IBM machine. But perhaps in a little while the distinctions will not be so clear. The moment we can do that we will have carried out a psychological experiment in new terms which for the first time may give a sharp definition of what is meant by a joke. (Edward Teller, 'Progress in the Nuclear Age', *Mayo Clinic Proceedings*, January 1965.)

> Can a computer be used to compose a symphony? As one who has been engaged in programming a large digital computer to program original musical compositions, I can testify that the very idea excites incredulity and indignation in many quarters. Such response in part reflects the extreme view of the nineteenth-century romantic tradition that regards music as direct communication of emotion from composer to listener – 'from heart to heart', as Wagner said. In deference to this view it must be conceded that we do not *yet* understand the subjective aspect of musical communication well enough to study it in precise terms. ... On the other hand, music does have its objective side. The information encoded there relates to such quantitative entities as pitch and time, and is therefore accessible to rational and ultimately mathematical analysis. ... it is possible, at least in theory, to construct tables of probabilities describing a musical style, such as Baroque, Classical or Romantic, and perhaps even the style of an individual composer. Given such tables, one could then reverse the process and compose music in a given style. (Lejaren A. Hiller, Jr., in *Scientific American*, December 1959. Italics added.)

The most ominous aspect of such statements is the ever-present 'yet' that appears in them. To offer another example: 'No technology as *yet* promises to duplicate human creativity, especially in the artistic sense, if only because we do not *yet* understand the conditions and functioning of creativity. (This is not to deny that computers can be useful aids to creative activity.)' (Emmanuel G. Mesthene, *How Technology Will Shape the Future*, Harvard University Program on Technology and Society, Reprint Number 5, pp.14–15.) The presumption involved in such statements is almost comic. For the man who thinks that creativity might *yet* become a technology is the man who stands no chance of ever understanding what creativity is. But we can be sure the technicians will eventually find us a bad mechanized substitute and persuade themselves that it is the real thing.

(6)   The literature of our society dealing with imprisonment and capital punishment is extensive, including contributions by Tolstoy, Camus, Dostoyevsky, Sartre, and Koestler. Since, however, these men offer us

only imaginative fiction, their work is obviously of little scientific value. What follows is an attempt by two psychiatrists to gain, at long last, some hard data on the experience of awaiting execution. The sample population is nineteen people in the Sing Sing death house. 'One might expect them', the researchers state, 'to show severe depression and devastating anxiety, yet neither symptom was conspicuous among these 19 doomed persons. By what mechanisms did they avoid these expected reactions to such overwhelming stress? Do their emotional patterns change during a year or two in a death cell? And do these defenses function to the moment of execution – or do they crumble towards the end?'

Here are the psychiatrists' thumbnail sketches of their specimens – all of whom, they observe, come from 'deprived backgrounds', with extensive experience of institutional confinement, and none of whom had long premeditated the killings they were convicted of. Notice how effectively the terminology and the data provided screen out the observer so that we have no sense of the character of the human presence with which these pathetic prisoners were interacting – surely a key factor in the situation. Note, too, how the concluding table of findings turns the life-and-death matter into a statistical abstraction.

> This inmate is the only woman in this series. She is of dull intelligence, acts in a playful and flirtatious manner. She was usually euphoric, but became transiently depressed when she thought her case was going badly. She frequently complained of insomnia and restlessness. These symptoms quickly disappeared when she was visited by a psychiatrist whom she enjoyed seeing and talking to in a self-justifying and self-pitying manner. Psychological tests showed pervasive feelings of insecurity, repressive defenses, and an inability to handle angry and aggressive feelings in an effectual manner.

> This inmate is an illiterate, inadequate individual who was convicted as an accomplice to a robbery-murder. He had an overall IQ of 51. He showed primarily depression, withdrawal, and obsessive rumination over the details of his crime and conviction. He eventually evolved a poorly elaborated paranoid system whereby he supposedly was betrayed and framed by his girl friend and one of the codefendants. Despite the looseness of his persecutory thinking, it was accompanied by a clear-cut elevation in his mood and reduction of anxiety.

> He is one of the two inmates in this series who uses religious preoccupation as his major defense mechanism. He repeatedly in an almost word for word way stated his situation as follows. 'No one can understand how I feel unless it happened to you. Christ came to me and I know He died for my sins. It doesn't matter if I am electrocuted or not. I am going to another world after this and I am prepared for it.' As his stay progresses he becomes increasingly more hostile and antagonistic, and his behavior progressively out of keeping with his professed religious ideas. In addition to obsessive rumination, projection and withdrawal are employed to ward off feelings of anxiety and depression.

The researchers summarize their findings as follows:

Psychological defense mechanisms used
(Totals more than 19; some used more than one)

Denial by isolation of affect	7
Denial by minimizing the predicament	4
Denial by delusion formation	1
Denial by living only in the present	4
Projection	7
Obsessive rumination in connection with appeals	3
Obsessive preoccupation with religion	2
Obsessive preoccupation with intellectual or philosophical matters	5

(Harvey Bluestone and Carl L. McGahee, 'Reaction to Extreme Stress: Impending Death by Execution', *The American Journal of Psychiatry*, November 1962, pp.393–96.)

(7)   Reportedly, within the last decade, the most promising scientific brains have been drifting away from physics to biology and medical science, where the frontiers of research have begun to reveal more intriguing prospects. Some of them, like that which follows, vie with the ingenuity of H.G. Wells' Dr Moreau.

Dr Vladimir Demikhov, an eminent Soviet experimental surgeon whose grafting of additional or different heads and limbs on to dogs has drawn considerable attention, has come up with a new suggestion for the advancement of transplantation surgery.

According to 'Soviet Weekly', Dr Demikhov believes that it would be simple to store organs for spare-part surgery – not by developing techniques for banks or particular organs or tissues but by temporarily grafting the stored organ on to the exterior of human 'vegetables'.

A human 'vegetable' is a human being who, through accident or disease, has lost all intelligent life, but is otherwise functioning normally. The surgeon's 'bank' would consist of technically living bodies, each supporting externally a number of additional organs. (Anthony Tucker, science correspondent, *The Guardian* [London], January 20, 1968.)

For a popularized survey of recent work in the biological sciences, see Gordon Rattray Taylor, *The Biological Time-Bomb* (New York: World, 1968). Among other breathtaking possibilities the biologists have in store for us, there will be the capacity to produce carbon-copy human beings with interchangeable parts and faultless collective co-ordination. We shall then have, we are told, 'exceptional human beings in unlimited numbers', as well as ideal basketball teams ... and (no doubt) armies.

(8)   The following are two examples of scientists doing their utmost to defend the dignity of pure research against any moralizing encroachments.

In December 1967, Dr Arthur Kornberg, a Nobel prize winning geneticist, announced the first successful synthesis of viral DNA, an important step toward the creation of test-tube life. After the announcement Dr Kornberg was interviewed by the press.

> At the end, the moral problem was posed. 'Dr Kornberg, do you see the time when your work will come into conflict with traditional morality?' Again he took off his glasses and looked down and meditated. Very gently, he replied: 'We can never predict the benefits that will flow from advancements in our fundamental knowledge. There is no knowledge that cannot be abused, but I hope that our improved knowledge of genetic chemistry will make us better able to cope with hereditary disease. I see no possibility of conflict in a decent society which uses scientific knowledge for human improvement.' ... He left it to us to define, or redefine, a decent society. (Alistair Cooke, reporting in *The Guardian* [London], December 17, 1967.)

In the summer of 1968, a controversy blew up in Great Britain over the part played by academic scientists in the activities of the Ministry of Defence Microbiological Establishment at Porton, one of the world's most richly productive centers of chemical and biological warfare research. (Porton, for example, developed some of the gases most extensively used by American forces in Vietnam.) Professor E.B. Chain of Imperial College protested this 'irresponsible scoop hunting' in a lengthy letter to *The Observer*, detailing the many worthwhile lines of research that had come out of the work done at Porton.

> What is wrong with accepting research grants from the Ministry of Defence? As is well known, thousands of scientists have, for many years, accepted such grants from the US Navy, the US Air Force, NATO, and similar national and international organisations for fundamental research in many branches of the physical and biological sciences: this does not mean that such work involved them in research on military technology. One can only be grateful for the wisdom and foresight shown by those responsible for formulating and deciding the policies of these organisations in allowing their funds to be made available for sponsoring fundamental university research which bears no immediate, and usually not even a remote, relation to problems of warfare technology.
>
> Of course, almost any kind of research, however academic, and almost any invention, however beneficial to mankind, from the knife to atomic energy, from anaesthetics to plant hormones, can be used for war and other destructive purposes, but it is, of course, not the scientist and inventor who carries the responsibility for how the results of his research or his inventions are used. (*The Observer* [London], June 1, 1968.)

It is actually a dubious proposition that any scientist worth his salt cannot make a pretty accurate prediction of how his findings might be used. But even if one were to grant the point, there is one kind of result which is completely predictable and which is bound never to be far from the awareness of the researcher. Productive research results in a handsomely rewarded career, in acclaim and wide recognition. Is it too cynical to suggest that this all-too-predictable result frequently makes it ever so much harder to foresee the probable abuses of one's research?

(9)   C. Wright Mills once called the middle class citizenry of our polity a collection of 'cheerful robots'. Perhaps it is because the human original has fallen so far short of authenticity that our behavioural scientists can place such easy confidence in the simulated caricatures of humanity upon which their research ever more heavily comes to bear. One begins to wonder how much of what our society comes to accept as humanly normal, legitimate, and appropriate in years to come will be patterned upon the behavior of such electronic homunculi as those described below.

> A pioneering demonstration of the feasibility of computer simulation appeared in 1957 when Newell, Shaw, and Simon published a description of their Logic Theorist program, which proved theorems in elementary symbolic logic – a feat previously accomplished only by humans. Among subsequent applications of information processing programs to classical problems of psychological theory are Feigenbaum's Elementary Perceiver and Memorizer, a computer model of verbal rote memorization; Feldman's simulation of the behavior of subjects in a binary-choice experiment, and Hovland and Hunt's model of human concept formulation. Lindsay explores another facet of cognitive activity in his computer processing of syntactic and semantic information to analyze communications in Basic English, and Bert Green and associates have programmed a machine to respond to questions phrased in ordinary English. Still another aspect of human decision-making appears in Clarkson's model of the trust investment process. At a more general level, Newell, Shaw, and Simon have programmed an information processing theory of human problem solving, a model whose output has been compared systematically with that of human problem solvers. Reitman has incorporated elements of this general problem-solving system in simulating the complex creative activity involved in musical composition.

> While early applications of information processing models focus on relatively logical aspects of human behavior, recent simulation models incorporate emotional responses. Concerned by the singlemindedness of cognitive activity programmed in the Newell, Shaw, and Simon General Problem Solver, Reitman and associates recently have programmed a Hebbian-type model of human thinking that is not in complete control of what it remembers and forgets, being subject to interruptions and to conflict. Kenneth Colby, a psychiatrist, has developed a computer model for simulating therapeutic manipulation of emotions as well as a patient's responses. In HOMUNCULUS, our computer model of elementary social behavior, simulated subjects may at times emit anger or guilt reactions, or they may suppress aggression and later vent it against a less threatening figure than the one who violated norms regarding distributive justice.

> ... Among other computer applications involving considerations of emotional behavior are Coe's simulation of responses to frustration and

conflict, Loehlin's simulation of socialization, and Abelson's design for computer simulation of 'hot', affect-laden cognition. Imaginative computer simulations of voting behavior have been done by Robert Abelson, William McPhee, and their associates. Using the fluoridation controversies as a case in point, Abelson and Bernstein blend theories from several disciplines and from both field and experimental phenomena in constructing their model. Simulated individuals are assigned characteristics known to be relevant, and the programmed model specifies the processes by which they may change during the fluoridation campaign. ...

In another study ... Raymond Breton has simulated a restriction-of-output situation. According to this model, under most conditions pressures from fellow workmen result in a more homogeneous output, presumably in conformity with the norm. When motivation for monetary reward is intensified, however, some simulated workers develop negative sentiments toward those attempting to apply constraints, and variability of output increases.

(J.T. and J.E. Gullahorn, 'Some Computer Applications in Social Science', *American Sociological Review*, vol. 30, June 1965, pp.353–365.)

B5 John C. Whitcomb, Jr, and Henry M. Morris, *The Genesis Flood*

From J.C. Whitcomb, Jr and H.M. Morris (1961) *The Genesis Flood: The Biblical Record and Its Scientific Implications*, Grand Rapids, Mich., Baker, 8th printing, pp.116–20, 327–30.

[T]he Biblical account of the Flood describes it as of global extent, both anthropologically and geographically. All non-geological objections to this plain teaching of Scripture have been considered and, we believe, thoroughly discredited. There seems to be no reasonable question that, if language can at all be used to convey sensible meanings, the writer of the account of the Deluge (supported by many later writers of Scripture and especially by the Lord Jesus Himself) definitely intended to record the great fact of a universal, world-destroying Flood, of absolute uniqueness in the entire history of this planet.

But [...] over the past century and more, the development of historical geology has been accompanied by a gradual rejection of the Scriptural revelation of the early history of the earth, at least in its geological implications. Except for occasional abortive attempts to harmonize the sequences of creation week with those of the geological ages, modern geology has all but universally repudiated the book of Genesis, as far as any geological significance is concerned. [...]

The Flood was once believed to be the explanation for most of the phenomena of geology; later it was regarded as one of a series of geological cataclysms which were the key features in geologic interpretation; then it was thought to explain only certain of the superficial deposits of the earth's surface; finally it was either dismissed as legendary or interpreted as a local flood in Mesopotamia, thus stripping it of all geological consequence. One may search modern geological textbooks or reference works from one end of the library to the other and find in every work consulted either no mention of the Noachian Flood at all or else perhaps a patronizing reference in some historical note on the rise of modern geology.

A Bible-believing Christian thus faces a serious dilemma. When many thousands of trained geologists, most of them sincere and honest in their conviction of the correctness of their interpretation of the geological data, present an almost unanimous verdict against the Biblical accounts of creation and the Flood, he must of course feel very reluctant to oppose such a tremendous array of scholarship and authority.

On the other hand, when confronted with the Biblical evidence for a global Flood, of tremendous geological potency, he is still more reluctant to reject the Bible's testimony. This is no problem, of course, to men who do not accept the inspiration of the Bible or the authority of Jesus Christ. But the instructed Christian knows that the evidences for full divine inspiration of Scripture are far weightier than the evidences for any fact of science. [...] The decision then must be faced: either the Biblical record of the Flood is false and must be rejected or else the system of historical geology which has seemed to discredit it is wrong and must be changed. The latter alternative would seem to be the only one which a Biblically and scientifically instructed Christian could honestly take, regardless of the 'deluge' of scholarly wrath and ridicule that taking such a position brings upon him. [...]

It becomes very important, therefore, for Christians to re-study and re-think the great mass of geologic and paleontologic data, with two main purposes in view. The first aim should be to examine carefully the currently accepted scheme of historical geology and its guiding principles, in order to determine clearly wherein and to what degree it is at variance with the Biblical record of creation and the Flood. If this scheme is basically fallacious, as we have had to decide it must be, then we need to try to understand why it could be that such a great body of responsible scientists has accepted it as true. It will be necessary also to discover and point out the inadequacies of the scheme from a strictly scientific viewpoint and to show that it is unable to correlate satisfactorily all the available geologic data. [...]

The second aim [...] will be to develop, if possible, a new scheme of historical geology, which would not only be true to the Biblical revelations that are pertinent to it but also would serve as a better basis of correlation for the available scientific data than does the present one.

These goals are, to put it very mildly, not easily attainable. It will likely have to be attempted, if at all, largely by men outside the camp of professional geologists. It is unlikely that many students majoring in the field could survive several years of intensive indoctrination in the uniformitarian interpretation of geology without becoming immune to any other interpretation and still less likely that they would ever be granted graduate degrees in this field without subscribing wholeheartedly to it. There is an immense amount of data available that must be restudied and re-evaluated, enough to require the attention of many experts for a very long period of time. Considering the dual limitations imposed on the present writers by their lack of broad training in this field and by the lack of available space in this volume, all that is hoped for at present is to develop and present a plausible preliminary outline study which will stimulate others to further study along the same lines.

[* * *]

Although there may be considerable latitude of opinion about details, the Biblical record *does* provide a basic outline of earth history, within which all the scientific data ought to be interpreted. It describes an initial Creation, accomplished by processes which no longer are in operation and which, therefore, cannot possibly be understood in terms of present physical or biological mechanisms. It describes the entrance into this initial Creation of the supervening principle of decay and deterioration: the 'curse' pronounced by God on the 'whole creation', resulting from the sin and rebellion of man, the intended master of the terrestrial economy, against his Creator.

The record of the great Flood plainly asserts that it was so universal and cataclysmic in its cause, scope and results that it also marked a profound hiatus in terrestrial history. Thus the Creation, the Fall, and the Flood constitute the truly basic facts, to which all the other details of early historical data must be referred.

Within this basic framework we have attempted to re-interpret the basic data of historical geology and other pertinent sciences, which at present are popularly interpreted in a context of uniformitarianism and evolutionism. We have tentatively suggested a categorization of the various geologic strata and formations in terms of the Biblical periods of earth history, although retaining as far as possible the terminology of the presently accepted geological periods.

Thus, it seems most reasonable to attribute the formations of the crystalline basement rocks, and perhaps some of the Pre-Cambrian non-fossiliferous sedimentaries, to the Creation period, though later substantially modified by the tectonic upheavals of the Deluge period. The fossil-bearing strata were apparently laid down in large measure during the Flood, with the apparent sequences attributed not to evolution but rather to hydrodynamic selectivity, ecologic habitats, and differential mobility and strength of the various creatures.

An undetermined amount of the strata, particularly in the upper levels, may have been reworked and redeposited during the later stages of the

Deluge, as a result of the great epeirogenic (continental uplift) processes which ended the universal inundation. These processes and the hydrologic abnormalities accompanying them evidently continued with gradually-lessening intensity for many centuries after the Flood. Thus, many of the geologic strata, especially those attributed to the Pleistocene, may actually have been laid down after the Flood, although related to residual catastrophism caused by the Flood. [...]

The Flood itself appears to have been due to a combination of meteorologic and tectonic phenomena. The 'fountains of the great deep' emitted great quantities of juvenile water and magmatic materials, and the 'waters above the firmament', probably an extensive thermal atmospheric blanket of water vapor, condensed and precipitated torrential rains for a period of forty days.

We realize that such a thorough reorganization of the geologic data raises many questions and must be subject to modification and revision in many details. Nevertheless, we believe that this type of analysis comes much more realistically to grips with all the basic data than does the commonly accepted theory of uniformitarianism.

But the latter theory will undoubtedly die hard, mainly because it is the chief bulwark of evolutionism, and evolution is the great 'escape mechanism' of modern man. This is the pervasive philosophic principle by which man either consciously or sub-consciously seeks intellectual justification for escape from personal responsibility to his Creator and escape from the 'way of the Cross' as the necessary and sufficient means of his personal redemption.

Numerous objections will, therefore, be raised to our exposition of Biblical-geological catastrophism, most of them ostensibly on the basis that various types of deposits and geologic phenomena are difficult to reconcile with Biblical chronology. [...] But, in the last analysis, it is likely that on questions so fundamental and basically emotional and spiritual as these, each man will continue to believe as he 'wants' to believe. We can only show that those who want to believe the Bible can do so in full confidence that the actual data of geology are consistent with such a belief, even though the apparent weight of scholarly opinion for the past century has been on the side of those who want to believe otherwise. [...]

The decision between alternate theories does not [...] depend only on the scientific data but is ultimately a moral and emotional decision. Dr Barrington Moore, senior research fellow at the Russian Research Center at Harvard University, has said:

> Few people today are likely to argue that the acceptance of scientific theories, even by scientists themselves, depends entirely upon the logical evidence adduced in support of these theories. Extraneous factors related to the philosophical climate and society in which the scientist lives always play at least some part [Barrington Moore, Jr.: 'Influence of Political Creeds on the Acceptance of Theories', *Scientific Monthly*, Vol. 79, September 1954, p.146].

We therefore urge the reader to face up to the fact that the actual data of geology *can* be interpreted in such a way as to harmonize quite effectively with a literal interpretation of the Biblical records and then also to recognize the spiritual implications and consequences of this fact.

B6 William R. Overton, 'Creationism in schools'

From [W.R. Overton] (1982) 'Creationism in schools: the decision in Mclean versus the Arkansas Board of Education', *Science*, vol. 215, pp.938–9.

The approach to teaching 'creation science' and 'evolution science' found in Act 590 is identical to the two-model approach espoused by the Institute for Creation Research and is taken almost verbatim from ICR writings. It is an extension of Fundamentalists' view that one must either accept the literal interpretation of Genesis or else believe in the godless system of evolution.

The two model approach of the creationists is simply a contrived dualism [...] which has no scientific factual basis or legitimate educational purpose. It assumes only two explanations for the origins of life and existence of man, plants and animals: It was either the work of a creator or it was not. Application of these two models, according to creationists, and the defendants, dictates that all scientific evidence which fails to support the theory of evolution is necessarily scientific evidence in support of creationism and is, therefore, creation science 'evidence' in support of Section 4(a). [...]

In addition to the fallacious pedagogy of the two model approach, Section 4(a) lacks legitimate educational value because 'creation science' as defined in that section is simply not science. Several witnesses suggested definitions of science. A descriptive definition was said to be that science is what is 'accepted by the scientific community' and is 'what scientists do'. The obvious implication of this description is that, in a free society, knowledge does not require the imprimatur of legislation in order to become science.

More precisely, the essential characteristics of science are:

(1) It is guided by natural law;

(2) It has to be explanatory by reference to natural law;

(3) It is testable against the empirical world;

(4) Its conclusions are tentative, i.e., are not necessarily the final word; and

(5) It is falsifiable. [...]

Creation science as described in Section 4(a) fails to meet these essential characteristics. First, the section revolves around 4(a) (1) which asserts a sudden creation 'from nothing'. Such a concept is not science because it depends upon a supernatural intervention which is not guided by natural law. It is not explanatory by reference to natural law, is not testable and is not falsifiable. [...]

If the unifying idea of supernatural creation by God is removed from Section 4, the remaining parts of the section explain nothing and are meaningless assertions.

Section 4(a) (2), relating to the 'insufficiency of mutation and natural selection in bringing about development of all living kinds from a single organism', is an incomplete negative generalization directed at the theory of evolution.

Section 4(a) (3) which describes 'changes only within fixed limits of originally created kinds of plants and animals' fails to conform to the essential characteristics of science for several reasons. First, there is no scientific definition of 'kinds' and none of the witnesses was able to point to any scientific authority which recognized the term or knew how many 'kinds' existed. One defense witness suggested there may be 100 to 10,000 different 'kinds'. Another believes there were 'about 10,000, give or take a few thousand'. Second, the assertion appears to be an effort to establish outer limits of changes within species. There is no scientific explanation for these limits which is guided by natural law and the limitations, whatever they are, cannot be explained by natural law.

The statement in 4(a) (4) of 'separate ancestry of man and apes' is a bald assertion. It explains nothing and refers to no scientific fact or theory. [...]

Section 4(a) (5) refers to 'explanation of the earth's geology by catastrophism, including the occurrence of a worldwide flood'. This assertion completely fails as science. The Act is referring to the Noachian flood described in the Book of Genesis. The creationist writers concede that *any* kind of Genesis Flood depends upon supernatural intervention. A worldwide flood as an explanation of the world's geology is not the product of natural law, nor can its occurrence be explained by natural law.

Section 4(a) (6) equally fails to meet the standards of science. 'Relatively recent inception' has no scientific meaning. It can only be given meaning by reference to creationist writings which place the age at between 6,000 and 20,000 years because of the genealogy of the Old Testament. [...] Such a reasoning process is not the product of natural law; not explainable by natural law; nor is it tentative.

Creation science, as defined in Section 4(a), not only fails to follow the canons defining scientific theory, it also fails to fit the more general descriptions of 'what scientists think' and 'what scientists do'. The scientific community consists of individuals and groups, nationally and internationally, who work independently in such varied fields as biology, paleontology, geology and astronomy. Their work is published and subject to review and testing by their peers. The journals for publication are both numerous and varied. There is, however, not one recognized scientific journal which has published an article espousing the creation science theory described in Section 4(a). Some of the State's witnesses suggested that the scientific community was 'close-minded' on the subject of creationism and that explained the lack of acceptance of the creation science arguments. Yet no witness produced a scientific article for which publication had been refused. Perhaps some members of the scientific community are resistant to new ideas. It is, however, inconceivable that such a loose knit group of independent thinkers in all the varied fields of science could, or would, so effectively censor new scientific thought. [...]

The methodology employed by creationists is another factor which is indicative that their work is not science. A scientific theory must be tentative and always subject to revision or abandonment in light of facts that are inconsistent with, or falsify, the theory. A theory that is by its own terms dogmatic, absolutist and never subject to revision is not a scientific theory.

The creationists' methods do not take data, weigh it against the opposing scientific data, and thereafter reach the conclusions stated in Section 4(a). Instead, they take the literal wording of the Book of Genesis and attempt to find scientific support for it. The method is best explained in the language of Morris in his book (Px 31) *Studies in The Bible and Science* at page 114:

> ... it is ... quite impossible to determine anything about Creation through a study of present processes, because present processes are not creative in character. If man wishes to know anything about Creation (the time of Creation, the duration of Creation, the order of Creation, the methods of Creation, or anything else) his sole source of true information is that of divine revelation. God was there when it happened. We were not there. ... Therefore, we are completely limited to what God has seen fit to tell us, and this information is in His written Word. This is our textbook on the science of Creation!

The Creation Research Society employs the same unscientific approach to the issue of creationism. Its applicants for membership must subscribe to the belief that the Book of Genesis is 'historically and scientifically true in all of the original autographs'. [...] The Court would never criticize or discredit any person's testimony based on his or her religious beliefs. While anybody is free to approach a scientific inquiry in any fashion they choose, they cannot properly describe the methodology used as scientific, if they start with a conclusion and refuse to change it regardless of the evidence developed during the course of the investigation.

B7 Lynn White, Jr, 'The historical roots of our ecologic crisis'

From L. White, Jr (1967) 'The historical roots of our ecologic crisis', *Science*, vol.155, pp.1203–4, 1205, 1206, 1207.

As we enter the last third of the 20th century [...] concern for the problem of ecologic backlash is mounting feverishly. Natural science, conceived as the effort to understand the nature of things, had flourished in several eras and among several peoples. Similarly there had been an age-old accumulation of technological skills, sometimes growing rapidly, sometimes slowly. But it was not until about four generations ago that Western Europe and North America arranged a marriage between science and technology, a union of the theoretical and the empirical approaches to our natural environment. The emergence in widespread practice of the Baconian creed that scientific knowledge means technological power over nature can scarcely be dated before about 1850, save in the chemical industries, where it is anticipated in the 18th century. Its acceptance as a normal pattern of action may mark the greatest event in human history since the invention of agriculture, and perhaps in nonhuman terrestrial history as well.

Almost at once the new situation forced the crystallization of the novel concept of ecology; indeed, the word *ecology* first appeared in the English language in 1873. Today, less than a century later, the impact of our race upon the environment has so increased in force that it has changed in essence. When the first cannons were fired, in the early 14th century, they affected ecology by sending workers scrambling to the forests and mountains for more potash, sulfur, iron ore, and charcoal, with some resulting erosion and deforestation. Hydrogen bombs are of a different order: a war fought with them might alter the genetics of all life on this planet. By 1285 London had a smog problem arising from the burning of soft coal, but our present combustion of fossil fuels threatens to change the chemisty of the globe's atmosphere as a whole, with consequences which we are only beginning to guess. With the population explosion, the carcinoma of planless urbanism, the now geological deposits of sewage and garbage, surely no creature other than man has ever managed to foul its nest in such short order.

There are many calls to action, but specific proposals, however worthy as individual items, seem too partial, palliative, negative: ban the bomb, tear down the billboards, give the Hindus contraceptives and tell them to eat their sacred cows. The simplest solution to any suspect change is, of course, to stop it, or, better yet, to revert to a romanticized past: make those ugly gasoline stations look like Anne Hathaway's cottage or (in the Far West) like ghost-town saloons. The 'wilderness area' mentality invariably advocates deep-freezing an ecology, whether San Gimignano or the High Sierra, as it was before the first Kleenex was dropped. But neither atavism not prettification will cope with the ecologic crisis of our time.

What shall we do? No one yet knows. Unless we think about fundamentals, our specific measures may produce new backlashes more serious than those they are designed to remedy.

As a beginning we should try to clarify our thinking by looking, in some historical depth, at the presuppositions that underlie modern technology and science. [...]

What people do about their ecology depends on what they think about themselves in relation to things around them. Human ecology is deeply conditioned by beliefs about our nature and destiny – that is, by religion. To Western eyes this is very evident in, say, India or Ceylon. It is equally true of ourselves and of our medieval ancestors.

The victory of Christianity over paganism was the greatest psychic revolution in the history of our culture. It has become fashionable today to say that, for better or worse, we live in 'the post-Christian age'. Certainly the forms of our thinking and language have largely ceased to be Christian, but to my eye the substance oftens remains amazingly akin to that of the past. Our daily habits of action, for example, are dominated by an implicit faith in perpetual progress which was unknown either to Greco-Roman antiquity or to the Orient. It is rooted in, and is indefensible apart from, Judeo-Christian teleology. The fact that Communists share it merely helps to show what can be demonstrated on many other grounds: that Marxism, like Islam, is a Judeo-Christian heresy. We continue today to live, as we have lived for about 1700 years, very largely in a context of Christian axioms.

What did Christianity tell people about their relations with the environment?

While many of the world's mythologies provide stories of creation, Greco-Roman mythology was singularly incoherent in this respect. Like Aristotle, the intellectuals of the ancient West denied that the visible world had had a beginning. Indeed, the idea of a beginning was impossible in the framework of their cyclical notion of time. In sharp contrast, Christianity inherited from Judaism not only a concept of time as nonrepetitive and linear but also a striking story of creation. By gradual stages a loving and all-powerful God had created light and darkness, the heavenly bodies, the earth and all its plants, animals, birds, and fishes. Finally, God had created Adam and, as an afterthought, Eve to keep man from being lonely. Man named all the animals, thus establishing his dominance over them. God planned all of this explicitly for man's benefit and rule: no item in the physical creation had any purpose save to serve man's purposes. And, although man's body is made of clay, he is not simply part of nature: he is made in God's image.

Especially in its Western form, Christianity is the most anthropocentric religion the world has seen. As early as the 2nd century both Tertullian and Saint Irenaeus of Lyons were insisting that when God shaped Adam he was foreshadowing the image of the incarnate Christ, the Second Adam. Man shares, in great measure, God's transcendence of nature. Christianity, in absolute contrast to ancient paganism and Asia's religions (except, perhaps, Zoroastrianism), not only established a dualism of man and nature but also insisted that it is God's will that man exploit nature for his proper ends.

At the level of the common people this worked out in an interesting way. In Antiquity every tree, every sping, every stream, every hill had its own *genius loci*, its guardian spirit. These spirits were accessible to men, but were very unlike men; centaurs, fauns, and mermaids show their ambivalence. Before one cut a tree, mined a mountain, or dammed a brook, it was important to placate the spirit in charge of that particular situation, and to keep it placated. By destroying pagan animism, Christianity made it possible to exploit nature in a mood of indifference to the feelings of natural objects. [...]

The Christian dogma of creation, which is found in the first clause of all the Creeds, has another meaning for our comprehension of today's ecologic crisis. By revelation, God had given man the Bible, the Book of Scripture. But since God had made nature, nature also must reveal the divine mentality. The religious study of nature for the better understanding of God was known as natural theology. In the early Church, and always in the Greek East, nature was conceived primarily as a symbolic system through which God speaks to men: the ant is a sermon to sluggards; rising flames are the symbol of the soul's aspiration. This view of nature was essentially artistic rather than scientific. While Byzantium preserved and copied great numbers of ancient Greek scientific texts, science as we conceive it could scarcely flourish in such an ambience.

However, in the Latin West by the early 13th century natural theology was following a very different bent. It was ceasing to be the decoding of the physical symbols of God's communication with man and was becoming the effort to understand God's mind by discovering how his creation operates. The rainbow was no longer simply a symbol of hope first sent to Noah after the Deluge: Robert Grosseteste, Friar Roger Bacon, and Theodoric of Freiberg produced startlingly sophisticated work on the optics of the rainbow, but they did it as a venture in religious understanding. From the 13th century onward, up to and including Leibnitz and Newton, every major scientist, in effect, explained his motivations in religious terms. Indeed, if Galileo had not been so expert an amateur theologian he would have got into far less trouble: the professionals resented his intrusion. And Newton seems to have regarded himself more as a theologian than as a scientist. It was not until the late

18th century that the hypothesis of God became unnecessary to many scientists.

It is often hard for the historian to judge, when men explain why they are doing what they want to do, whether they are offering real reasons or merely culturally acceptable reasons. The consistency with which scientists during the long formative centuries of Western science said that the task and the reward of the scientist was 'to think God's thoughts after him' leads one to believe that this was their real motivation. If so, then modern Western science was cast in a matrix of Christian theology. The dynamism of religious devotion, shaped by the Judeo-Christian dogma of creation, gave it impetus.

We would seem to be headed toward conclusions unpalatable to many Christians. Since both *science* and *technology* are blessed words in our contemporary vocabulary, some may be happy at the notions, first, that, viewed historically, modern science is an extrapolation of natural theology and, second, that modern technology is at least partly to be explained as an Occidental, voluntarist realization of the Christian dogma of man's transcendence of, and rightful mastery over, nature. But, as we now recognize, somewhat over a century ago science and technology – hitherto quite separate activities – joined to give mankind powers which, to judge by many of the ecologic effects, are out of control. If so, Christianity bears a huge burden of guilt.

I personally doubt that disastrous ecologic backlash can be avoided simply by applying to our problems more science and more technology. Our science and technology have grown out of Christian attitudes toward man's relation to nature which are almost universally held not only by Christians and neo-Christians but also by those who fondly regard themselves as post-Christians. Despite Copernicus, all the cosmos rotates around our little globe. Despite Darwin, we are *not*, in our hearts, part of the natural process. We are superior to nature, contemptuous of it, willing to use it for our slightest whim. The newly elected Governor of California, like myself a churchman but less troubled than I, spoke for the Christian tradition when he said (as is alleged), 'when you've seen one redwood tree, you've seen them all'. To a Christian a tree can be no more than a physical fact. The whole concept of the sacred grove is alien to Christianity and to the ethos of the West. For nearly 2 millennia Christian missionaries have been chopping down sacred groves, which are idolatrous because they assume spirit in nature.

What we do about ecology depends on our ideas of the man-nature relationship. More science and more technology are not going to get us out of the present ecologic crisis until we find a new religion, or rethink our old one. The beatniks, who are the basic revolutionaries of our time, show a sound instinct in their affinity for Zen Buddhism, which conceives of the man-nature relationship as very nearly the mirror image of the Christian view. Zen, however, is as deeply conditioned by Asian history as Christianity is by the experience of the West, and I am dubious of its viability among us.

Possibly we should ponder the greatest radical in Christian history since Christ: Saint Francis of Assisi. The prime miracle of Saint Francis is the fact that he did not end at the stake as many of his left-wing followers did. He was so clearly heretical that a General of the Franciscan Order, Saint Bonaventura, a great and perceptive Christian, tried to suppress the early accounts of Franciscanism. The key to an understanding of Francis is his belief in the virtue of humility – not merely for the individual but for man as a species. Francis tried to depose man from his monarchy over creation and set up a democracy of all God's creatures. With him the ant is no longer simply a homily for the lazy, flames a sign of the thrust of the soul toward union with God; now they are Brother Ant and Sister Fire, praising the Creator in their own ways as Brother Man does in his. [...]

[T]he present increasing disruption of the global environment is the product of a dynamic technology and science which were originating in the Western medieval world against which Saint Francis was rebelling in so original a way. Their growth cannot be understood historically apart from distinctive attitudes toward nature which are deeply grounded in Christian dogma. The fact that most people do not think of these attitudes as Christian is irrelevant. No new set of basic values has been accepted in our society to displace those of Christianity. Hence we shall continue to have a worsening ecologic crisis until we reject the Christian axiom that nature has no reason for existence save to serve man.

The greatest spiritual revolutionary in Western history, Saint Francis, proposed what he thought was an alternative Christian view of nature and man's relation to it: he tried to substitute the idea of the equality of all creatures, including man, for the idea of man's limitless rule of creation. He failed. Both our present science and our present technology are so tinctured with orthodox Christian arrogance toward nature that no solution for our ecologic crisis can be expected from them alone. Since the roots of our trouble are so largely religious, the remedy must also be essentially religious, whether we call it that or not. We must rethink and refeel our nature and destiny. The profoundly religious, but heretical, sense of the primitive Franciscans for the spiritual autonomy of all parts of nature may point a direction. I propose Francis as a patron saint for ecologists.

B8 Garrett Hardin, 'The tragedy of the commons'

From G. Hardin (1968) 'The tragedy of the commons', *Science*, vol.162, pp.1244, 1245, 1246, 1248.

We can make little progress in working toward optimum population size until we explicitly exorcize the spirit of Adam Smith in the field of practical demography. In economic affairs, *The Wealth of Nations* (1776) popularized the 'invisible hand', the idea that an individual who 'intends only his own gain', is, as it were, 'led by an invisible hand to promote ... the public interest'. Adam Smith did not assert that this was invariably true, and perhaps neither did any of his followers. But he contributed to a dominant tendency of thought that has ever since interfered with positive action based on rational analysis, namely, the tendency to assume that decisions reached individually will, in fact, be the best decisions for an entire society. If this assumption is correct it justifies the continuance of our present policy of laissez-faire in reproduction. If it is correct we can assume that men will control their individual fecundity so as to produce the optimum population. If the assumption is not correct, we need to reexamine our individual freedoms to see which ones are defensible.

[i]

The rebuttal to the invisible hand in population control is to be found in a scenario first sketched in a little-known pamphlet in 1833 by a mathematical amateur named William Forster Lloyd (1794–1852). We may well call it 'the tragedy of the commons', using the word 'tragedy' as the philosopher Whitehead used it: 'The essence of dramatic tragedy is not unhappiness. It resides in the solemnity of the remorseless working of things.' He then goes on to say, 'This inevitableness of destiny can only be illustrated in terms of human life by incidents which in fact involve unhappiness. For it is only by them that the futility of escape can be made evident in the drama.'

The tragedy of the commons develops in this way. Picture a pasture open to all. It is to be expected that each herdsman will try to keep as many cattle as possible on the commons. Such an arrangement may work reasonably satisfactorily for centuries because tribal wars, poaching, and disease keep the numbers of both man and beast well below the carrying capacity of the land. Finally, however, comes the day of reckoning, that is, the day when the long-desired goal of social stability becomes a reality. At this point, the inherent logic of the commons remorselessly generates tragedy.

As a rational being, each herdsman seeks to maximize his gain. Explicitly or implicitly, more or less consciously, he asks, 'What is the utility *to me* of adding one more animal to my herd?' This utility has one negative and one positive component.

1   The positive component is a function of the increment of one animal. Since the herdsman receives all the proceeds from the sale of the additional animal, the positive utility is nearly +1.

2   The negative component is a function of the additional overgrazing created by one more animal. Since, however, the effects of overgrazing are shared by all the herdsmen, the negative utility for any particular decision-making herdsman is only a fraction of –1.

Adding together the component partial utilities, the rational herdsman concludes that the only sensible course for him to pursue is to add another animal to his herd. And another; and another ... But this is the conclusion reached by each and every rational herdsman sharing a commons. Therein is the tragedy. Each man is locked into a system that compels him to increase his herd without limit – in a world that is limited. Ruin is the destination toward which all men rush, each pursuing his own best interest in a society that believes in the freedom of the commons. Freedom in a commons brings ruin to all.

Some would say that this is a platitude. Would that it were! [...] A simple incident that occurred a few years ago in Leominster, Massachusetts, shows how perishable the knowledge is. During the Christmas shopping season the parking meters downtown were covered with plastic bags that bore tags reading: 'Do not open until after Christmas. Free parking courtesy of the mayor and city council.' In other words, facing the prospect of an increased demand for already scarce space, the city fathers reinstituted the system of the commons. (Cynically, we suspect that they gained more votes than they lost by this retrogressive act.)

In an approximate way, the logic of the commons has been understood for a long time, perhaps since the discovery of agriculture or the invention of private property in real estate. But it is understood mostly only in special cases which are not sufficiently generalized. Even at this late date, cattlemen leasing national land on the western ranges demonstrate no more than an ambivalent understanding, in constantly pressuring federal authorities to increase the head count to the point where overgrazing produces erosion and weed-dominance. Likewise, the oceans of the world continue to suffer from the survival of the philosophy of the commons. Maritime nations still respond automatically to the shibboleth of the 'freedom of the seas'. Professing to believe in the 'inexhaustible resources of the oceans', they bring species after species of fish and whales closer to extinction.

The National Parks present another instance of the working out of the tragedy of the commons. At present, they are open to all, without limit. The parks themselves are limited in extent – there is only one Yosemite Valley – whereas population seems to grow without limit. The values that visitors seek in the parks are steadily eroded. Plainly, we must soon cease to treat the parks as commons or they will be of no value to anyone.

What shall we do? We have several options. We might sell them off as private property. We might keep them as public property, but allocate the right to enter them. The allocation might be on the basis of wealth, by the use of an auction system. It might be on the basis of merit, as defined by some agreed-upon standards. It might be by lottery. Or it might be on a first-come, first-served basis, administered to long queues. These, I think, are all the reasonable possibilities. They are all objectionable. But we must choose – or acquiesce in the destruction of the commons that we call our National Parks.

[ii]

In a reverse way, the tragedy of the commons reappears in problems of pollution. Here it is not a question of taking something out of the commons, but of putting something in – sewage, or chemical, radioactive, and heat wastes into water; noxious and dangerous fumes into the air; and distracting and unpleasant advertising signs into the line of sight. The calculations of utility are much the same as before. The rational man finds that his share of the cost of the wastes he discharges into the commons is less than the cost of purifying his wastes before releasing them. Since this is true for everyone, we are locked into a system of 'fouling our own nest', so long as we behave only as independent, rational, free-enterprisers.

The tragedy of the commons as a food basket is averted by private property, or something formally like it. But the air and waters surrounding us cannot readily be fenced, and so the tragedy of the commons as a cesspool must be prevented by different means, by coercive laws or taxing devices that make it cheaper for the polluter to treat his pollutants than to discharge them untreated. We have not progressed as far with the solution of this problem as we have with the first. Indeed, our particular concept of private property, which deters us from exhausting the positive resources of the earth, favors pollution. The owner of a factory on the bank of a stream – whose property extends to the middle of the stream – often has difficulty seeing why it is not his natural right to muddy the waters flowing past his door. The law, always behind the times, requires elaborate stitching and fitting to adapt it to this newly perceived aspect of the commons.

The pollution problem is a consequence of population. It did not much matter how a lonely American frontiersman disposed of his waste. 'Flowing water purifies itself every 10 miles', my grandfather used to say, and the myth was near enough to the truth when he was a boy, for there were not too many people. But as population became denser, the natural chemical and biological recycling processes became overloaded, calling for a redefinition of property rights. [...]

[iii]

The tragedy of the commons is involved in population problems in another way. In a world governed solely by the principle of 'dog eat dog' – if indeed there ever was such a world – how many children a family had would not be a matter of public concern. Parents who bred too exuberantly would leave fewer descendants, not more, because they would be unable to care adequately for their children. David Lack and others have found that such a negative feedback demonstrably controls the fecundity of birds. But men are not birds, and have not acted like them for millenniums, at least.

If each human family were dependent only on its own resources; *if* the children of improvident parents starved to death; *if*, thus, overbreeding brought its own 'punishment' to the germ line – *then* there would be no public interest in controlling the breeding of families. But our society is deeply committed to the welfare state, and hence is confronted with another aspect of the tragedy of the commons.

In a welfare state, how shall we deal with the family, the religion, the race, or the class (or indeed any distinguishable and cohesive group) that adopts overbreeding as a policy to secure its own aggrandizement? To couple the concept of freedom to breed with the belief that everyone born has an equal right to the commons is to lock the world into a tragic course of action. [...]

[iv]

Perhaps the simplest summary of this analysis of man's population problems is this: the commons, if justifiable at all, is justifiable only under conditions of low-population density. As the human population has increased, the commons has had to be abandoned in one aspect after another.

First we abandoned the commons in food gathering, enclosing farm land and restricting pastures and hunting and fishing areas. These restrictions are still not complete throughout the world.

Somewhat later we saw that the commons as a place for waste disposal would also have to be abandoned. Restrictions on the disposal of domestic sewage are widely accepted in the Western world; we are still struggling to close the commons to pollution by automobiles, factories, insecticide sprayers, fertilizing operations, and atomic energy installations.

In a still more embryonic state is our recognition of the evils of the commons in matters of pleasure. There is almost no restriction on the propagation of sound waves in the public medium. The shopping public is assaulted with mindless music, without its consent. Our government is paying out billions of dollars to create supersonic transport which will disturb 50,000 people for every one person who is whisked from coast to coast 3 hours faster. Advertisers muddy the airwaves of radio and television and pollute the view of travellers. We are a long way from outlawing the commons in matters of pleasure. [...]

Every new enclosure of the commons involves the infringement of somebody's personal liberty. Infringements made in the distant past are accepted because no contemporary complains of a loss. It is the newly proposed infringements that we vigorously oppose; cries of 'rights' and 'freedom' fill the air. But what does 'freedom' mean? When men mutually agreed to pass laws against robbing, mankind became more free, not less so. Individuals locked into the logic of the commons are free only to bring on universal ruin; once they see the necessity of mutual coercion, they become free to pursue other goals. I believe it was Hegel who said, 'Freedom is the recognition of necessity.'

The most important aspect of necessity that we must now recognize, is the necessity of abandoning the commons in breeding. No technical solution can rescue us from the misery of overpopulation. Freedom to breed will bring ruin to all. At the moment, to avoid hard decisions many of us are tempted to propagandize for conscience and responsible parenthood. The temptation must be resisted, because an appeal to independently acting consciences selects for the disappearance of all conscience in the long run, and an increase in anxiety in the short.

The only way we can preserve and nurture other and more precious freedoms is by relinquishing the freedom to breed, and that very soon. 'Freedom is the recognition of necessity' – and it is the role of education to reveal to all the necessity of abandoning the freedom to breed. Only so, can we put an end to this aspect of the tragedy of the commons.

B9 Anon., 'Transformation'

From G. De Bell (ed.) (1970) *The Environmental Handbook: Prepared for the First National Environmental Teach-in*, New York, Ballantine/Friends of the Earth, pp.330–33.

The condition

Position: Everyone is the result of four forces – the conditions of this known-universe (matter/energy forms, and ceaseless change); the biology of his species; his individual genetic heritage; and the culture he's born into. Within this web of forces there are certain spaces and loops which allow total freedom and illumination. The gradual exploration of some of these spaces is 'evolution' and, for human cultures, what 'history' could be. We have it within our deepest powers not only to change our 'selves' but to change our culture. If a man is to remain on earth he must transform the five-millenia long urbanizing civilization tradition into a new ecologically-sensitive harmony-oriented wild-minded scientific/spiritual culture. 'Wildness is the state of complete awareness. That's why we need it.'

Situation: civilization, which has made us so successful a species, has overshot itself and now threatens us with its inertia. There is some evidence that civilized life isn't good for the human gene pool. To achieve the changes we must change the very foundations of our society and our minds.

Goal: nothing short of total transformation will do much good. What we envision is a planet on which the human population lives harmoniously and dynamically by employing a sophisticated and unobtrusive technology in a world environment which is 'left natural'. Specific points in this vision:

- A healthy and spare population of all races, much less in number than today.

- Cultural and individual pluralism, unified by a type of world tribal council. Division by natural and cultural boundaries rather than arbitrary political boundaries.

- A technology of communication, education, and quiet transportation, land-use being sensitive to the properties of each region. Allowing, thus, the bison to return to much of the high plains. Careful but intensive agriculture in the great alluvial valleys; deserts left wild for those who would trot in them. Computer technicians who run the plant part of the year and walk along with the Elk in their migrations during the rest.

- A basic cultural outlook and social organization that inhibits power and property-seeking while encouraging exploration and challenge in things like music, meditation, mathematics, mountaineering, magic, and all other ways of authentic being-in-the-world. Women totally free and equal. A new kind of family – responsible, but more festive and relaxed – is implicit.

Action

Social/political: It seems evident that there are throughout the world certain social and religious forces which have worked through history toward an ecologically and culturally enlightened state of affairs. Let these be encouraged: Gnostics, hip Marxists, Teilhard de Chardin Catholics, Druids, Taoists, Biologists, Witches, Yogins, Bhikkus, Quakers, Sufis, Tibetans, Zens, Shamans, Bushmen, American Indians, Polynesians, Anarchists, Alchemists ... the list is long. All primitive cultures, all communal and ashram movements. Since it doesn't seem practical or even desirable to think that direct bloody force will achieve much, it would be best to consider this a continuing 'revolution of consciousness' which will be won not by guns but by seizing the key images, myths, archetypes, eschatologies, and ecstasies so that life won't seem worth living unless one's on the transforming energy's side. By taking over 'science and technology' and releasing its real possibilities and powers in the service of this planet – which, after all, produced us and it.

Our community. New schools, new classes, walking in the woods and cleaning up the streets. Find psychological techniques for creating an awareness of 'self' which includes the social and natural environment. 'Consideration of what specific language forms – symbolic systems – and social institutions constitute obstacles to ecological awareness.' Without falling into a facile interpretation of McLuhan, we can hope to use the media. Let no one be ignorant of the facts of biology and related disciplines; bring up our children as part of the wild-life. Some communities can establish themselves in backwater rural areas and flourish – others maintain themselves in urban centers, and the two types work together – a two-way flow of experience, people, money, and home-grown vegetables. Ultimately cities will exist only as joyous tribal gatherings and fairs, to dissolve after a few weeks. Investigating new life-styles is our work, as is the exploration of Ways to explore our inner realms – with the known dangers of crashing that go with such. We should work with political-minded people where it helps, hoping to enlarge their vision, and with people of all varieties of politics or thought at whatever point they become aware of environmental urgencies. Master the archaic and the primitive as models of basic nature-related cultures – as well as the most imaginative extensions of science – and build a community where these two vectors cross.

Our own heads: is where it starts. Knowing that we are the first human beings in history to have all of man's culture and previous experience available to our study, and being free enough of the weight of traditional cultures to seek out a larger identity. – The first members of a civilized society since the early neolithic to wish to look clearly into the eyes of the wild and see our selfhood, our family, there. We have these advantages to set off the obvious disadvantages of being as screwed up as we are – which gives us a fair chance to penetrate into some of the riddles of ourselves and the universe, and to go beyond the idea of 'man's survival' or 'the survival of the biosphere' and to draw our strength from the realization that at the heart of things is some kind of serene and ecstatic process which is actually beyond qualities and certainly beyond birth-and-death. 'No need to survive!' 'In the fires that destroy the universe at the end of the kalpa, what survives?' – 'The iron tree blooms in the void!'

Knowing that nothing need be done, is where we begin to move from.

Section C RELIGION AND COUNTER-CULTURES

C1 Theodore Roszak, 'Journey to the East ... and points beyond'

From T. Roszak (1970 edn) *The Making of a Counter Culture: Reflections on the Technocratic Society and Its Youthful opposition*, London, Faber & Faber, Chapter 4, pp.138–9, 140, 141, 142–3, 144–7, 148, footnotes omitted, first published 1969.

Even more important is the social fact: Ginsberg the mantra-chanting Hindu does not finish as an isolated eccentric, but rather as one of the foremost spokesmen of our younger generation. Following Ginsberg, the young don cowbells, tuck flowers behind their ears, and listen entranced to the chants. And through these attentive listeners Ginsberg claims a greater audience among our dissenting youth than any Christian or Jewish clergyman could hope to reach or stir. [...]

Indeed, we are a post-Christian era – despite the fact that minds far more gifted than Ginsberg's, like that of the late Thomas Merton, have mined the dominant religious tradition for great treasures. But we may have been decidedly wrong in what we long expected to follow the death of the Christian God; namely, a thoroughly secularized, thoroughly positivistic culture, dismal and spiritless in its obsession with technological prowess. That was the world Aldous Huxley foresaw in the 1930s, when he wrote *Brave New World*. But in the 1950s, as Huxley detected the rising spirit of a new generation, his utopian image brightened to the forecast he offers us in *Island* where a non-violent culture elaborated out of Buddhism and psychedelic drugs prevails. It was as if he had suddenly seen the possibility emerge: what lay beyond the Christian era and the 'wasteland' that was its immediate successor might be a new, eclectic religious revival. Which is precisely what confronts us now as one of the massive facts of the counter culture. The dissenting young have indeed got religion. Not the brand of religion Billy Graham or William Buckley would like to see the young crusading for – but religion nonetheless. What began with Zen has now rapidly, perhaps too rapidly, proliferated into a phantasmagoria of exotic religiosity.

Who would have predicted it? At least since the Enlightenment, the major thrust of radical thought has always been anti-religious, if not openly, defiantly atheistic – perhaps with the exception of the early Romantics. And even among the Romantics, the most pious tended to become the most politically reactionary; for the rest, the Romantic project was to abstract from religion its essential 'feeling' and leave contemptuously behind its traditional formulations. Would-be Western revolutionaries have always been strongly rooted in a militantly skeptical secular tradition. The rejection of the corrupted religious establishment has carried over almost automatically into a root-and-branch rejection of all things spiritual. So 'mysticism' was to become one of the dirtiest words in the Marxist vocabulary. Since Diderot, the priest has had only one thing the radical wanted: his guts, with which to strangle the last king. [...]

But now, if one scans any of the underground weeklies, one is apt to find their pages swarming with Christ and the prophets, Zen, Sufism, Hinduism, primitive shamanism, theosophy, the Left-Handed Tantra. ... The Berkeley 'wandering priest' Charlie (Brown) Artman, who was in the running for city councilman in 1966 until he was arrested for confessing (quite unabashedly) to possession of narcotics, strikes the right note of eclectic religiosity: a stash of LSD in his Indian-sign necklace, a chatelaine of Hindu temple bells, and the campaign slogan 'May the baby Jesus open your mind and shut your mouth.' Satanists and Neo-Gnostics, dervishes and self-proclaimed swamis ... their number grows and the counter culture makes generous place for them. No anti-war demonstration would be complete without a hirsute, be-cowbelled contingent of holy men, bearing joss sticks and intoning the Hare Krishna. [...]

At the level of our youth, we begin to resemble nothing so much as the cultic hothouse of the Hellenistic period, where every manner of mystery and fakery, ritual and rite, intermingled with marvelous indiscrimination. [...]

What the counter culture offers us, then, is a remarkable defection from the long-standing tradition of skeptical, secular intellectuality which has served as the prime vehicle for three hundred years of scientific and technical work in the West. Almost overnight (and astonishingly, with no great debate on the point) a significant portion of the younger generation has opted out of that tradition, rather as if to provide an emergency balance to the gross distortions of our technological society, often by occult aberrations just as gross. As often happens, one cultural exaggeration calls forth another, which can be its opposite, but equivalent. [...]

Expertise – technical, scientific, managerial, military, educational, financial, medical – has become the prestigious mystogogy of the technocratic society. Its principal purpose in the hands of ruling elites is to mystify the popular mind by creating illusions of omnipotence and omniscience – in much the same way that the pharaohs and priesthood of ancient Egypt used their monopoly of the calendar to command the awed docility of ignorant subjects. Philosophy, the hard-headed Wittgenstein once said, is the effort to keep ourselves from being hexed by language. But largely under the influence of logicians and technicians, and with the supposed purpose of de-hexing our thinking, we have produced the scientized jargon which currently dominates official parlance and the social sciences. When knowledgeable men talk, they no longer talk of substances and accidents, of being and spirit, of virtue and vice, of sin and salvation, of deities and demons. Instead, we have a vocabulary filled with nebulous quantities of things that have every appearance of precise calibration, and decorated with vaguely mechanistic-mathematical terms like 'parameters', 'structures', 'variables', 'inputs and outputs', 'correlations', 'inventories', 'maximizations', and 'optimizations'. The terminology derives from involuted statistical procedures and methodological mysteries to which only graduate education gives access. The more such language and numerology one packs into a document, the more 'objective' the document becomes – which normally means the less morally abrasive to the sources that have subsidized the research or to any sources that might conceivably subsidize one's research at any time in the future. The vocabulary and the methodology mask the root ethical assumptions of policy or neatly transcribe them into a depersonalized rhetoric which provides a gloss of military or political necessity. To think and to talk in such terms becomes the sure sign of being a certified realist, a 'hard research' man.

Thus to bomb more hell out of a tiny Asian country in one year than was bombed out of Europe in the whole Second World War becomes 'escalation'. Threatening to burn and blast to death several million civilians in an enemy country is called 'deterrence'. Turning a city into radioactive rubble is called 'taking out' a city. A concentration camp (already a euphemism for a political prison) becomes a 'strategic hamlet'. A comparison of the slaughter on both sides in a war is called a 'kill ratio'. Totaling up the corpses is called a 'body count'. Running the blacks out of town is called 'urban renewal'. Discovering ingenious new ways to bilk the public is called 'market research'. Outflanking the discontent of employees is called 'personnel management'. [...]

Governments have no doubt always resorted to such linguistic camouflage to obscure realities. Certainly the vice is not limited to our own officialdom. Marcuse has shrewdly shown how the Soviet Union's endlessly reiterated verbal formulae – 'warmongering capitalist imperialism', 'the people's democratic' this or that, always the same adjective hitched to the same noun – use the Marxist lexicon to produce the same ritualistic obfuscations [Marcuse, *Soviet Marxism: A Critical Analysis*, p.88]. But the special irony of our situation is the employment of what purports to be a clinically objective vocabulary of technologisms for the purpose of hexing intelligence all over again.

When science and reason of state become the handmaidens of political black magic, can we blame the young for diving headlong into an occult Jungian stew in search of 'good vibrations' that might ward off the bad? Of course, they are soon glutted with what they find. They swallow it whole – and the result can be an absurdly presumptuous confabulation. Whole religious traditions get played with like so many baubles. A light-show group in Detroit names itself The Bulging Eyeballs of Gautama and the Beatles become the contemplative converts of a particularly simple-minded swami who advertises his mystic wares in every London underground station – only to drop him after a matter of months like a *passé* fashion.

No, the young do not by and large understand what these traditions are all about. One does not unearth the wisdom of the ages by shuffling about a few exotic catch phrases – nor does one learn anything about anybody's lore or religion by donning a few talismans and dosing on LSD. The most that comes of such superficial muddling is something like Timothy Leary's brand of easy-do syncretism: 'somehow' all is one – but never mind precisely how. [...] In the turgid floodtide of discovery, sampling, and restive fascination, perhaps it would be too much to expect disciplined order of the young in their pursuit – and surely it would be folly to try to deduce one from their happy chaos. They have happened upon treasure-trove long buried and are busy letting the quaint trinkets spill through their fingers.

For all its frequently mindless vulgarity, for all its tendency to get lost amid the exotic clutter, there is a powerful and important force at work in this wholesale willingness of the young to scrap our culture's entrenched prejudice against myth, religion, and ritual. The life of Reason (with a capital R) has all too obviously failed to bring us the agenda of civilized improvements the Voltaires and Condorcets once foresaw. Indeed, Reason, material Progress, the scientific world view have revealed themselves in numerous respects as simply a higher superstition, based on dubious but well-concealed assumptions about man and nature. Science, it has been said, thrives on sins of omission. True enough; and for three hundred years, those omissions have been piling up rather like the slag tips that surround Welsh mining towns: immense, precipitous mountains of frustrated human aspiration which threaten dangerously to come cascading down in an impassioned landslide. It is quite impossible any longer to ignore the fact that our conception of intellect has been narrowed disastrously by the prevailing assumption, especially in the academies, that the life of the spirit is: (1) a lunatic fringe best left to artists and marginal visionaries; (2) an historical boneyard for antiquarian scholarship; (3) a highly specialized adjunct of professional anthropology; (4) an antiquated vocabulary still used by the clergy, but intelligently soft-pedaled by its more enlightened members. Along none of these approaches can the living power of myth, ritual, and rite be expected to penetrate the intellectual establishment and have any existential (as opposed to merely academic) significance. If conventional scholarship does touch these areas of human experience, it is ordinarily with the intention of compiling knowledge, not with the hope of salvaging value.

When academics and intellectuals arrogantly truncate the life of the mind in this way, we finish with that 'middle-class secular humanism' of which Michael Novak has aptly said,

> It thinks of itself as humble in its agnosticism, and eschews the 'mystic flights' of metaphysicians, theologians and dreamers; it is cautious and

remote in dealing with heightened and passionate experiences that are the stuff of great literature and philosophy. It limits itself to this world and its concerns, concerns which fortunately turn out to be largely subject to precise formulations, and hence have a limited but comforting certainty.

[M. Novak, 'God in the colleges: the dehumanization of the university' in Cohen and Hale, *The New Student Left*, pp.253–65.]

I think we can anticipate that in the coming generation, large numbers of students will begin to reject this reductive humanism, demanding a far deeper examination of that dark side of the human personality which has for so long been written off by our dominant culture as 'mystical'. It is because this youthful renaissance of mythical-religious interest holds such promise of enriching our culture that one despairs when, as so often happens, the young reduce it in their ignorance to an esoteric collection of peer-group symbols and slogans, vaguely daring and ultimately trivial. [...]

For what they are groping their way toward through all their murky religiosity is an absolutely critical distinction. The truth of the matter is: no society, not even our severely secularized technocracy, can ever dispense with mystery and magical ritual. These are the very bonds of social life, the inarticulate assumptions and motivations that weave together the collective fabric of society and which require periodic collective affirmation. But there is one magic that seeks to open and vitalize the mind, another that seeks to diminish and delude. There are rituals which are imposed from on high for the sake of invidious manipulation; there are other rituals in which men participate democratically for the purpose of freeing the imagination and exploring self-expression. There are mysteries which, like the mysteries of state, are no better than dirty secrets; but there are also mysteries which are encountered by the community (if such exists) in a stance of radical equality, and which are meant to be shared in for the purpose of enriching life by experiences of awe and splendor.

C2 Lowell D. Streiker, 'The cults are coming!'

From L.D. Streiker, (1983 edn) *Cults: The Continuing Threat*, Nashville, Abingdon Press, pp.8–9, 13–15, first published in 1970 as *The Cults Are Coming!*

The cults are coming – to your city – to your neighborhood – to the family next door – to your family – to your life!

An invasion is under way. Beachheads have already been established in communities throughout America. Strange ideas, exotic practices, peculiar attitudes, unfamiliar modes of speech – these are some characteristics of the invaders.

The cults are coming. The advocates of all manner of spiritual disciplines are at the door. They are in our midst. Exaggerated depictions of their practices and powers fill popular literature, motion picture screens, newspapers, and television. *Rosemary's Baby, The Exorcist, The Omen, Carrie*, and the like appeal to our deepest sense of dread, our gut feeling that something is wrong with our world and that we are menaced by forces beyond ourselves – malevolent, capricious, and vicious forces.

The cults are here. Some of our friends, our friends' children, our own children, have been estranged from us by the Children of God or the Hare Krishnas or the Moonies or the self-proclaimed saviour-gods from the Orient. Many of us are involved in what we consider harmless flirtations with astrology, transcendental meditation, and spiritualism. Most of us would never forsake our spiritual heritage or way of life for a weird religious fringe group any more than we would give up our job and social identity to live by our wits and exertions in the wilds of some distant land. But aren't we attracted somehow by every new promise of peace of mind, of emotional closeness to other human beings, of a future filled with hope and fulfillment? [...]

Everyone has borrowed the language and style of the hippies. '*Get high* – daily existence is dull; so find the excitement of a 'peak experience'. *Tune in* – get in touch with your deepest feelings, with the world that surrounds you. *Drop out* – flaunt your distinctiveness against the forces that bind you to sterile conventions and rigid social roles. *End all downers* – change your way of living once and for all. Follow us and we will show you the true path to ecstatic self-fulfillment.' So say psychodrama retreats, feminist groups, encounter sessions, assertiveness training, transcendental meditation, Primal Therapy, holistic health, Scientology, biofeedback, massage workshops, et cetera, ad infinitum. The list grows and grows.

Examine the use of this overworked language by two religious groups:

> We are love revolutionaries stoned on Jesus the liberator. We are no longer hung up on materialism. We have beat the system. We find Jesus neat, a gas, out of sight. We groove on God, experience his life-style, and find a permanent high. Jesus is the ultimate trip.

> *Stay high forever.* No more coming down. Practice Krishna Consciousness. Expand your consciousness by practising the Transcendental Sound Vibration. Hare Krishna, Hare Krishna, ... Hare Hare. ... Try it and be blissful all the time. *Turn on* through music, dance, philosophy, science, religion, and prasadam (spiritual food). *Tune in.* Awaken your Transcendental Nature! ... *Drop out* of movements employing artificially induced states of self-realization and expanded consciousness. ... End all bringdowns, flip out and stay for eternity.

The first quotation comes from the followers of the Jesus movement. The second is the message of Krishna Consciousness. To some observers, these statements represent sophisticated efforts on the part of new religious movements to translate their message into contemporary forms. To me, they are advertising copy reminiscent of television commercials for pain relievers. They simply try too hard to catch the attention of their potential audience. But whether I like their propaganda or not, it is working.

C3 Eileen Barker, 'Numbers of movements'

From E. Barker (1989) *New Religious Movements: A Practical Introduction*, HMSO, Appendix 2, pp.148–55, footnotes omitted.

Numbers of movements

The actual number of NRMs in Britain depends upon the definition used [...] but a figure of around five hundred is not unreasonable. Claims have been made that there are up to 5,000 'cults' in North America, but no one has produced a list of these movements, and anyone who tried to do so would undoubtedly be using a very broad definition – a figure somewhere between 1,500 and 2,000 might be more realistic.

The Institute for the Study of American Religion, which houses one of the most comprehensive collections of data on American religion, has knowledge of a total of 1,667 different religious groups in North America; of these, 836 are classified as nonconventional religions. The Institute does *not* include movements which do not fall under the definition of religion used by the Institute, but which are sometimes called 'cults'. Examples would be *est*, Primal Therapy or Rebirthing. Of the nonconventional movements recognised as such by the Institute, around 500 were founded between 1950 and 1988.

If one turns to countries other than those in the West, a task not attempted in this book, the numbers of movements do, of course, increase enormously. Harold Turner has estimated that there could be over 10,000 new religious movements in Africa alone; and several hundred, if not several thousand, more could be added to the list if one were to include the movements in Asia (particularly Japan and Korea), the sub-continent of India, the Pacific Islands, South America and the West Indies.

There are around thirty new religious movements in the West about which a considerable amount of systematically researched information is available; there exists a growing collection of somewhat fragmentary information about a further two hundred or so of the movements; but there is, as yet, only the scantiest of information available to any but their members about the rest of the movements. The literature is extremely variable in content, but the total number of books and articles written on the subject during the past twenty years must be well into five figures – Peter Clarke and Elizabeth Arweck have, so far, collected 8,000 entries for an annotated bibliography that they are preparing at the Centre for New Religious Movements at King s College, London; John Saliba cites nearly 2,000 books and papers written from a psychological perspective; and Michael Mickler has compiled a list of 1,826 pieces of literature produced by or about the Unification Church alone.

Counting members in Britain

An obvious problem, which is related to that discussed in the previous sections, arises when one tries to estimate the total numbers of people involved in NRMs: a decision has to have been made as to what constitutes an NRM. Furthermore, even when one is attempting to count the number of members of a particular NRM, it is important to recognise the enormous diversity in the degree and type of membership that the movements may demand of their followers.

Most NRMs (like most mainstream Churches) have different 'layers' of membership, ranging from full-time service (equivalent to a priesthood), to active followers (similar to devout lay members of a congregation), with yet others who may be classified as constituting a mildly involved band of sympathisers. Another complication is that some people, especially those who have pursued a course with more than one of the self-religions, are quite likely to be counted several times as they move from one path to another. Bearing these problems in mind, what follows can be no more than a tentative attempt to give some idea of the membership of the movements in so far as such information is available.

In Britain, it is unlikely that any of the NRMs has succeeded, at any one time. in accumulating more than a few hundred members who devote their whole lives to working for their movement. It is impossible to estimate the number of people who, while living in their own homes and employed in an 'outside' job are deeply committed, and devote almost all of their spare time to a particular group or movement – rather like, in some ways, the elders or those who organise or devotedly attend the functions of their local church. If, however, an estimate were to be made, it would be likely to be somewhere in the tens of thousands. A greater number of people maintain a more peripheral relationship, which may. none the less, be of considerable importance in their lives. An even greater number will have come into contact with one or other of the movements for a short, transitory period. It is not impossible for members to change the level of their involvement according to their personal circumstances – for example, student (CARP) members of the Unification Church could become either full-time or associate members upon completing their studies.

There could be a million or so people who have, minimally, 'dabbled in' or 'flirted with' one or other of the movements in Britain at some time during the past quarter century. If one were to accept the claim that there is 'a conservative estimated population of over 250,000 Witches/Pagans

throughout the UK and many more hundreds of thousands of people
with a serious interest in Astrology, Alternative Healing Techniques and
Psychic Powers', and if one were to count such people as members of
NRMs, the total could be considerably greater.

Perhaps half a million have gone so far as to participate in a seminar,
course or workshop or to spend at least several hours investigating an
NRM. Half of these people could, however, be accounted for by their
having taken part in no more than a short course with either
Transcendental Meditation or the Church of Scientology. A spokesman
for Elan Vital (previously the Divine Light Mission) has said that around
20,000 persons have 'received the Knowledge' in Britain; *est* claims to
have had 8,000 'graduates' during its time in Britain – an equal number
may now have graduated from its successor, the Forum, and other related
seminars – and it is estimated that around 7,000 persons went through
the Exegesis seminar; other movements such as Insight/MSIA,
Psychosynthesis, the Rajneesh Foundation, Rebirthing, the School of
Economic Science and Self-Transformation Seminars have possibly had
4–7,000 doing one of their courses.

The Unification Church has about 350 full-time 'Core' members in Britain
(roughly two-thirds of whom are British); a further 100 or so 'Practising'
members, while not working full-time for the movement, accept the
teachings and attend services and donate money on a regular basis; and
about 8,000 people have signed an 'Associate membership' form –
although less than one in ten of these have any continuing contact with
the movement. The number of British Unificationists world-wide is
unknown, but it does not exceed 600, and may be well under 500.

In Britain, around 1,000 'students' practise Raja Yoga, but only about
eight work for the Brahma Kumaris movement on a full-time basis.
Nichiren Shoshu Buddhism has four thousand members who have
received their Gohonzon, but less than ten full-time staff members.
Between 1,200 to 1,400 people are said to practise the 'latihan' twice a
week with fellow members of Subud. There are about 300 names on the
Raëlians' mailing list, but reportedly only a dozen or so are committed
followers.

Other movements with probably more than a hundred, but less than a
thousand, fully committed members in Britain include the Aetherius
Society, the Children of God (Family of Love), ECKANKAR, the Emin
Foundation, Friends of the Western Buddhist Order, and Sahaja Yoga.
The Ananda Marga has a large following in India, but only a few hundred
associated members and no more than 30 or so full-time Margiis in
Britain. The Jesus Fellowship has 950 members, 600 of whom live in one
or other of their residential communities. There are about 150 Emissaries
of Divine Light, 60 of whom live in their Cotswold community. ISKCON
(the 'Hare Krishna' movement) has several tens of thousands of members
of the Asian community associated with it, but only about 300 full-time

devotees. There could be 10,000 or so followers of Saytha Sai Baba, the overwhelming majority belonging to the Asian community.

Perhaps the confusion that sometimes arises about what exactly is meant by membership and, consequently, about the numbers of people 'involved' in the movements can be further illustrated by looking in a bit more detail at the different kinds of involvement that exist in two movements that have had a relatively large number of people associated with them at some point: Transcendental Meditation and the Church of Scientology.

TM's Office of Information and Inspiration says that about 150,000 people in Britain have learned TM during a 4-day course, with about 6,000 more people currently taking the course every year. A total of around 2,500 have proceeded to the advanced 'TM-Sidhi Programme'. Most of these people have continued to lead 'ordinary lives' in that they neither work for nor reside with the movement, although an unknown number of them devote some time to meditation each day. However, some of those who practise the advanced TM-Sidhi Programme will, while remaining in outside jobs, have moved to live in the movement's 'Ideal Village' in Skelmersdale, Lancashire, which now has around 400 residents and a day school for about 80 of the residents' children. About 350 Meditators have pursued the techniques to train as TM teachers; of these, about 40 have a full-time career as TM teachers and a further 60 or so will teach on a part-time basis. About 40 people are engaged in various projects at Mentmore Towers, a further 8 or so are 'working for charity' at the movement's residential academy in Kent. Altogether there are around 100 people working full-time for TM in Britain.

The Church of Scientology says that, since it started offering courses in Britain in the early 1950s, around one hundred thousand people have paid for at least one of their introductory courses, which normally take place over a weekend. Only a very small proportion of these people will end up devoting their lives to the movement; at the time of writing, the movement has about 250 full-time staff members at its headquarters in East Grinstead, and about the same number of staff members spread around other centres throughout the country.

The point to be stressed is that, although some hundreds of thousands of individuals may have been classified as a 'member' of an NRM at some time during the past quarter of a century, the number of people whose involvement in an NRM results in their having greatly reduced contact with the rest of the world because they are living in a centre or working full-time for a movement is very small. In 1985, Beckford estimated that there had never been more than 15,000 committed members in Britain at any point in the previous decade.

The relevance of these figures so far as this book is concerned lies in the fact that it is the actions of the fully committed members, and the effect that full commitment can have on an individual's life that gives rise to most of the worries that have been expressed in relation to the NRMs. As suggested earlier, worries are seldom expressed about the tens of thousands of people of Asian origin who are associated with the Hare Krishna movement and who attend the movement's Temples for worship. The parents who become anxious are those whose sons or daughters become one of the few hundred Anglo-Saxon devotees who have dedicated their entire lives to Krishna Consciousness. Similarly, it is not the 8,000 or so people who have signed a Unification membership form who are going to change their lives in any significant way, but the 300 or so 'Core' members residing in Britain who will be significantly affected by their Unification membership.

A few further points ought to be made about the interpretation (or, more often, misinterpretation) of statistics when attempts to discern trends are made by the unwary – or by those who are overly eager to make a particular point. First, a *relative rate* of change in membership will be affected by the *absolute number* from which calculation starts (that is, how far the starting number is from zero). Secondly, the direction and strength of a trend will be affected by the *dates* that are chosen (for example, a closer look at a number of different points over a long period may reveal a cyclical pattern, a long-term trend that is not the same as a short-term trend, or a previous trend that has been reversed). Thirdly, when assessing the rate of *growth* of a movement, it is necessary to take account not only of conversion, but also of *defection*. Fourthly, care needs to be taken that one is measuring the same phenomenon when comparing change over time. Suppose, for example, the British membership of a movement were to be counted by itself to produce a statistic, then, at a later date, both the British and the Japanese membership of the movement were taken together to produce a second statistic. The fact that the second statistic was greater than the first could not be taken to indicate that either the British membership or the movement as a whole had increased in size. Fifthly, it is necessary to make sure that the statistics from which any inference about trends is being made are accurate.

All these rather obvious, but perhaps somewhat abstract, pitfalls can be illustrated in a more practical way by reference simply to one recent television programme which was introduced with the statement that fringe religions are steadily increasing their membership. As 'evidence', it went on to report that:

> The growth rate of the cults is phenomenal. According to the Christian Handbook, in 1970 the Moonies had just 50 followers in Britain; today they have 500. At the same time, the Scientologists had 10,000 followers; today they have 50,000 ...

As the Unification Church had only just started up in Britain in 1970, almost any increase would be bound to seem enormous when presented as it was on the programme by a histogram (a column representing 50 in 1970 was compared with one representing 450 in 1989) – while a similar addition of 450 members to the 516,739 recorded Methodists, or even the 107,767 Jehovah's Witnesses, would be quite undetectable. Turning to the trend, or pattern of the statistics, the number of Unificationists in Britain actually reached a peak of over a thousand (well under half of whom were British) in 1978 when several hundred members of the 'International One World Crusade' were sent to Britain on an evangelising mission. With the departure of the Crusade in 1981, it is hardly surprising that the number of Unificationists in Britain dropped; and the number continued to fall as British members were sent on overseas missions. However, the number of members actually joining in Britain has since then been matched by the number leaving the movement. This has meant that, throughout the 1980s, there has been a fairly stable situation so far as the 'British Family' is concerned – the 'British Family' being those who join the Unification Church in Britain – whatever their nationality. It might also be mentioned (although the programme did not do so) that the figure of 500 is given in the Handbook as an editorial estimate. The grounds for such an estimate is not immediately obvious as the Handbook's table reports a fall in membership from 570 in 1980 to 350 in 1985.

So far as the Scientology statistics are concerned, the way in which the movement's membership figures are recorded can, by itself, account for the increase. This is because, generally speaking, 'turn-over' does not affect the figures – anyone who has proceeded beyond a basic introductory course is counted as a member and is unlikely ever to be removed from the count. This means that even if, in any one year, 100 people ceased being associated with the movement and 10 people were to start being associated, the figures would give the misleading impression that there had been an increase rather than a fall in membership.

Of course, small, even declining, membership figures do not imply that new religious movements are socially insignificant – other sections of society are indirectly affected by their beliefs and practices. Nor, indeed, do such figures mean that the movements are not of fundamental concern to certain categories of people who, although themselves not members of a movement, have become affected through, for example, the involvement of a relative or friend. The small numbers of fully involved persons should, none the less, be borne in mind when considering the place of the movements in British society.

C4 Aldous Huxley, *The Doors of Perception*

From A. Huxley (1954) *The Doors of Perception*, London, Chatto and Windus, pp.59–63.

I am not so foolish as to equate what happens under the influence of mescalin or of any other drug, prepared or in the future preparable, with the realization of the end and ultimate purpose of human life: Enlightenment, the Beatific Vision. All I am suggesting is that the mescalin experience is what Catholic theologians call 'a gratuitous grace', not necessary to salvation but potentially helpful and to be accepted thankfully, if made available. To be shaken out of the ruts of ordinary perception, to be shown for a few timeless hours the outer and the inner world, not as they appear to an animal obsessed with survival or to a human being obsessed with words and notions, but as they are apprehended, directly and unconditionally, by Mind at Large – this is an experience of inestimable value to everyone and especially to the intellectual. [...]

Literary or scientific, liberal or specialist, all our education is predominantly verbal and therefore fails to accomplish what it is supposed to do. Instead of transforming children into fully developed adults, it turns out students of the natural sciences who are completely unaware of Nature as the primary fact of experience, it inflicts upon the world students of the Humanities who know nothing of humanity, their own or anyone else's. [...]

All sorts of cultists and queer fish teach all kinds of techniques for achieving health, contentment, peace of mind; and for many of their hearers many of these techniques are demonstrably effective. But do we see respectable psychologists, philosophers and clergymen boldly descending into those odd and sometimes malodorous wells, at the bottom of which poor Truth is so often condemned to sit? Yet once more the answer is, No.

And now look at the history of mescalin research. Seventy years ago men of first-rate ability described the transcendental experiences which come to those who, in good health, under proper conditions and in the right spirit, take the drug. How many philosophers, how many theologians, how many professional educators have had the curiosity to open this Door in the Wall? The answer, for all practical purposes, is, None.

In a world where education is predominantly verbal, highly educated people find it all but impossible to pay serious attention to anything but words and notions. There is always money for, there are always doctorates in, the learned foolery of research into what, for scholars, is the all-important problem: Who influenced whom to say what when? Even in this age of technology the verbal Humanities are honoured. The non-verbal humanities, the arts of being directly aware of the given facts of our existence, are almost completely ignored. A catalogue, a bibliography, a definitive edition of a third-rate versifier's *ipsissima verba*, a stupendous index to end all indexes – any genuinely Alexandrian project is sure of approval and financial support. But when it comes to finding out how you and I, our children and grandchildren, may become more perceptive, more intensely aware of inward and outward reality, more open to the Spirit, less apt, by psychological malpractices, to make ourselves physically ill, and more capable of controlling our own autonomic nervous system – when it comes to any form of non-verbal education more fundamental (and more likely to be of some practical use) than Swedish Drill, no really respectable person in any really respectable university or church will do anything about it. Verbalists are suspicious of the non-verbal; rationalists fear the given, non-rational fact; intellectuals feel that 'what we perceive by the eye (or in any other way) is foreign to us as such and need not impress us deeply'. Besides, this matter of education in the non-verbal Humanities will not fit into any of the established pigeon-holes. It is not religion, not neurology, not gymnastics, not morality or civics, not even experimental psychology. This being so, the subject is, for academic and ecclesiastical purposes, non-existent and may safely be ignored altogether or left, with a patronizing smile, to those whom the Pharisees of verbal orthodoxy call cranks, quacks, charlatans and unqualified amateurs. [...]

Systematic reasoning is something we could not, as a species or as individuals, possibly do without. But neither, if we are to remain sane, can we possibly do without direct perception, the more unsystematic the better, of the inner and outer worlds into which we have been born. This given reality is an infinite which passes all understanding and yet admits of being directly and in some sort totally apprehended. It is a transcendence belonging to another order than the human, and yet it may be present to us as a felt immanence, an experienced participation. To be enlightened is to be aware, always, of total reality in its immanent otherness – to be aware of it and yet to remain in a condition to survive as an animal, to think and feel as a human being, to resort whenever expedient to systematic reasoning. Our goal is to discover that we have always been where we ought to be. [...]

Near the end of his life Aquinas experienced Infused Contemplation. Thereafter he refused to go back to work on his unfinished book. Compared with *this*, everything he had read and argued about and written – Aristotle and the Sentences, the Questions, the Propositions, the majestic Summas – was no better than chaff or straw. For most intellectuals such a sit-down strike would be inadvisable, even morally wrong. But the Angelic Doctor had done more systematic reasoning than any twelve ordinary Angels, and was already ripe for death. He had earned the right, in those last months of his mortality, to turn away from merely symbolic straw and chaff to the bread of actual and substantial Fact. For Angels of a lower order and with better prospects of longevity, there must be a return to the straw. But the man who comes back through the Door in the Wall will never be quite the same as the man who went out. He will be wiser but less cocksure, happier but less self-satisfied, humbler in acknowledging his ignorance yet better equipped to understand the relationship of words to things, of systematic reasoning to the unfathomable Mystery which it tries, forever vainly, to comprehend.

C5 Timothy Leary, Autobiography

From T. Leary (1968) *High Priest*, New York, World, pp.2–3.

Trip 1

In the beginning God created the heavens and the earth.

The earth was without form and void, and darkness was on the face of the deep.

*

Nicholas in *The Magus* by John Fowles:

For a while I let my mind wander into a bottomless madness.

Supposing all my life that last year had been the very opposite of what Conchis so often said – so often, to trick me once again – about life in general.

That is, the very opposite of hazard.

*

And God said let there be light; and there was light. And God saw that the light was good; and God separated the light from the darkness.

In the beginning was the TURN ON. The flash, the illumination. The electric trip. The sudden bolt of energy that starts the new system.

The TURN ON was God.

All things were made from the TURN ON and without Him was not any thing made.

In this TURN ON was life, and the life was the light of men.

It has always been the same.

It was the flash that exploded the galaxies, from which all energy flows. It was the spark that ignites in the mysterious welding of amino acid strands that creates the humming vine of organic life. It is the brilliant neurological glare that illuminates the shadows of man's mind. The God intoxicated revelation. The Divine union. The vision of harmony, samadhi, satori, ecstasy which we now call psychedelic.

What happens when you turn on? Where do you go when you take the trip? You go within. Consciousness changes. Your nerve endings, neural cameras, cellular memory banks, protein structures become broadcasting instruments for the timeless humming message of God located inside your body.

The external world doesn't change, but your experience of it becomes drastically altered.

You close your eyes and the thirteen billion cell brain computer flashes multiple kaleidoscopic messages. Symbolic thought merges with sensory explosions; symbolic thoughts fuse with somatic-tissue events; ideas combine with memories – personal, cellular, evolutionary, embryonic – thoughts collapse into molecular patterns.

You open your eyes and you see your tidy television-studio world of labeled stage props fusing with sensory, somatic, cellular, molecular flashes.

Nicholas in *The Magus:*

I stared at myself. They were trying to drive me mad, to brainwash me in some astounding way. But I clung to reality.

*

And God saw that it was good.

*

From *The Magus:*

I cannot believe Maurice is evil. You will understand.

*

And God made the beasts of the earth according to their kinds and the cattle

according to their kinds and everything that creeps upon the ground according to its kind. And God saw that it was good.

*

Your nervous system is prepared to register and coordinate up to one thousand million units of flashing information each second.

A psychedelic trip lasts from five to twelve hours. Each trip takes off from a stage-set structured by the physical surroundings and the cast of characters present. Each person in the session is a universe of two billion years of protein, protean memories, and sensations. A heady mix.

How to describe this multiple, jumbled, rapidly changing process? What do you do after you TURN ON?

The Light shineth in the darkness and the darkness comprehendeth it not.

You TUNE IN.

TUNE IN means to bear witness to the Light, that all men might believe.

The TURN ON bolt shatters structure. Reveals the frozen nature of the artificial stage-set men call reality. Certitude collapses. There is nothing but the energy which lighteneth every man that cometh into the world. $E = MC^2$.

We discover we are not television actors born onto the American stage-set of a commercially sponsored program twenty centuries old. We are two-billion-year-old carriers of the Light, born not just of blood nor of the will of the flesh, nor of the will of man, but of the Light that flashed in the Precambrian mud, the Light made flesh.

TUNE IN means that you sit in the debris of your shattered illusions, and discover that there is nothing, you are nothing except the bearer of the wire-coil of life, that your body is the temple of the Light and you begin once again to build a structure to preserve and glorify the Light. You bear witness crying, the Sun that comes after me is preferred before me, and your days are spent preparing the earth for the Son to come. That is TUNING IN.

And to TUNE IN you must DROP OUT.

DROP OUT means detach yourself tenderly, aesthetically, harmoniously from the fake-prop studio of the empire game and do nothing but guard and glorify the Light.

C6   Timothy Leary, 'Start your own religion'

From T. Leary (1968) *The Politics of Ecstasy*, New York, The League for Spiritual Discovery, pp.222–32.

The Purpose of Life is Religious Discovery

That intermediate manifestation of the divine process which we call the DNA code has spent the last 2 billion years making this planet a Garden of Eden. An intricate web has been woven, a delicate fabric of chemical-electrical-seed-tissue-organism-species. A dancing, joyous harmony of energy transactions is rooted in the 12 inches of topsoil which covers the rock

metal

fire

core of this planet.

Into this Garden of Eden each human being is born perfect. We were all born divine mutants, the DNA code's best answer to joyful survival on this planet. An exquisite package for adaptation based on 2 billion years of consumer research (RNA) and product design (DNA).

But each baby, although born perfect, immediately finds himself in an imperfect, artificial, disharmonious social system which systematically robs him of his divinity.

And the social systems – where did they come from?

Individual societies begin in harmonious adaptation to the environment and, like individuals, quickly get trapped into non-adaptive, artificial, repetitive sequences.

When the individual's behavior and consciousness get hooked to a routine sequence of external actions, he is a dead robot

and

When the individual's behavior and consciousness get hooked to a routine sequence of external actions, he is a dead robot,

and

When the individual's behaviour and consciousness get hooked to a routine sequence of external actions, he is a dead robot and it is time for him to die and be reborn. Time to 'drop out', 'turn on', and 'tune in'. This period of robotization is called the Kali Yuga, the Age of Strife and Empire, the peak of so-called civilization, the Johnson Administration, etc. This relentless law of death, life, change is the rhythm of the galaxies and the seasons, the rhythm of the seed. It never stops.

Drop Out. Turn On. Tune In.

Drop Out – detach yourself from the external social drama which is as dehydrated and ersatz as TV.

Turn On – find a sacrament which returns you to the temple of God, your own body. Go out of your mind. Get high.

Tune In – be reborn. Drop back in to express it. Start a new sequence of behavior that reflects your vision.

But the sequence must continue. You cannot stand still.

Death. Life. Structure.

D. L. S.

D. L. S. D. L. S. D.

L. S. D. L. S. D. L.

S. D. L. S. D. ...

Any action that is not a conscious expression of the drop-out-turn-on-tune-in-drop-out rhythm is the dead posturing of robot actors on the fake-prop TV studio stage set that is called American reality.

Actions which are conscious expressions of the turn-on, tune-in, drop-out rhythm are religious.

The wise person devotes his life exclusively to the religious search – for therein is found the only ecstasy, the only meaning.

Anything else is a competitive quarrel over (or Hollywood-love sharing of) television studio props.

How to Turn On

To turn on is to detach from the rigid addictive focus on the fake-prop TV studio set and to refocus on the natural energies within the body.

To turn on, you go out of your mind and:

1. Come to your senses – focus on sensory energies.

2. Resurrect your body – focus on somatic energies.

3. Drift down cellular memory tracks beyond the body's space-time – focus on cellular energies.

4. Decode the genetic code.

Note well: at each of these levels (sensory, somatic, cellular, molecular), attention can be directed at energy changes within or without the body. If attention is directed externally during the session, the outside world is experienced in terms of a non-symbolic energy-language focus. Be careful. This can be shocking. The props of the TV studio stage set are suddenly experienced:

1. As sensory (e.g., the room is alive, out of control, exploding with light and sound)

2. As somatic (e.g., the room is alive, undulating with digestive rhythm)

3. As cellular (e.g., all props and actors take on a stylized, mythic, reincarnate hue)

4. As molecular (e.g., all props and actors shimmer impersonally as vibratory mosaics)

Recognition eliminates fear and confusion. To turn on, you need maps and manuals.

To turn on, you must learn how to pray. Prayer is the compass, the gyroscope for centering and stillness.

Turning on is a complex, demanding, frightening, confusing process. It requires diligent yoga.

Turning on requires a guide who can center you at the TV-stage-prop level and at the sensory, somatic, cellular, and molecular levels.

When you turn on, remember: you are not a naughty boy getting high for kicks.

You are a spiritual voyager furthering the most ancient, noble quest of man. When you turn on, you shed the fake-prop TV studio and costume and join the holy dance of the visionaries. You leave LBJ and Bob Hope; you join Lao-tse, Christ, Blake. Never underestimate the sacred meaning of the turn-on.

To turn on, you need a sacrament. A sacrament is a visible external thing which turns the key to the inner doors. A sacrament must bring about bodily changes. A sacrament flips you out of the TV-studio game and harnesses you to the 2-billion-year-old flow inside.

A sacrament which works is dangerous to the establishment which runs the fake-prop TV studio – and to that part of your mind which is hooked to the studio game.

Each TV-prop society produces exactly that body-changing sacrament which will flip out the mind of the society.

Today the sacrament is LSD. New sacraments are coming along.

Sacraments wear out. They become part of the social TV-studio game. Treasure LSD while it still works. In fifteen years it will be tame, socialized, and routine.

How to Tune In

You cannot stay turned on all the time. You cannot stay any place all the time. That's a law of evolution. After the revelation it is necessary to drop back in, return to the fake-prop TV studio and initiate small changes which reflect the glory and the meaning of the turn-on. You change the way you move, the way you dress, and you change your corner of the TV-studio society. You begin to look like a happy saint. Your home slowly becomes a shrine. Slowly, gently, you start seed transformations around you. Psychedelic art. Psychedelic style. Psychedelic music. Psychedelic dance.

Suddenly you discover you have dropped out.

How to Drop Out

Drop out means exactly that: drop out.

Most of the activity of most Americans goes into robot performances on the TV-studio stage. Fake. Unnatural. Automatic.

Drop out means detach yourself from every TV drama which is not in the rhythm of the turn-on, tune-in, drop-out cycle.

Quit school. Quit your job. Don't vote. Avoid all politics. Do not waste conscious thinking on TV-studio games. Political choices are meaningless.

To postpone the drop-out is to cop out.

Dismiss your fantasies of infiltrating the social stage-set game. Any control you have over television props is their control over you.

Dismiss the Judaic-Christian-Marxist-puritan-literary-existentialist suggestion that the drop-out is escape and that the conformist cop-out is reality. Dropping out is the hardest yoga of all.

Make your drop-out invisible. No rebellion – please!

To Drop Out, You Must Form Your Own Religion

The drop-out, turn-on, tune-in rhythm is most naturally done in small groups of family members, lovers, and seed friends.

For both psychedelic and legal reasons, you must form your own cult.

The directors of the TV studio do not want you to live a religious life. They will apply every pressure (including prison) to keep you in their game.

Your own mind, which has been corrupted and neurologically damaged by years of education in fake-prop TV-studio games, will also keep you trapped in the game.

A group liberation cult is required.

You must form that most ancient and sacred of human structures – the clan. A clan or cult is a small group of human beings organized around a religious goal.

Remember, you are basically a primate. You are designed by the 2-billion-year blueprint to live in a small band.

You cannot accept the political or spiritual leadership of anyone you cannot touch, con-spire (breathe) with, worship with, get high with.

Your clan must be centered on a shrine and a totem spiritual energy source. To the clan you dedicate your highest loyalty, and to you the clan offers its complete protection.

But the clan must be centered on religious goals. Religion means being tuned in to the natural rhythm. Religion is the turn-on, tune-in, drop-out process.

Because you and your clan brothers are turned on, you will radiate energy. You will attract attention – hostility from the TV establishment, enthusiastic interest from rootless TV actors who wish to join your clan. Everyone basically wants to turn on, tune in, and drop out.

Avoid conflict with the establishment. Avoid recruiting and rapid growth. Preserve clan harmony.

Your clan must be limited to essential friends.

You must guard against the TV power tendency toward e x p a n s i o n.

Your clan cannot become a mail-order, mass-numbers organization.

The structure of your clan must be cellular.

The center of your religion must be a private, holy place.

The activities of your religion must be limited to the turn-on, tune-in, drop-out sequence. Avoid commitments to TV-studio power games.

You must start your own religion. You are God – but only you can discover and nurture your divinity. No one can start your religion for you.

In particular, those Americans who use psychedelic chemicals – marijuana, peyote, LSD – must appraise their goals and games realistically. You smoke pot? Good. But why? As part of your personality game? As part of the American TV-studio perspective? To enhance your ego? As part of your TV role as hipster, sophisticate, rebel? Because it is the in-thing to do in your stage set? Because it is a social-psychological habit? Good. Keep on. The 'pot game' is a fascinating scenario to act out, the entertaining game of illicit kicks.

There is another way of viewing psychedelic drugs, including pot: from the perspective of history. For thousands of years the greatest artists, poets, philosophers, and lovers have used consciousness-expanding substances to turn on, tune in, drop out. As part of the search for the meaning of life. As tools to reach new levels of awareness. To see beyond the immediate social game. For revelation. For light in the darkness of the long voyage.

Every great burst of activity has grown out of a psychedelic turn-on. The visionary then rushes back to tune in, to pass on the message. A new art form. A new mode of expression. He turns others on. A cult is formed. A new TV stage set is designed, one that is closer to the family clan-tribal cell structure of our species.

Do you wish to use marijuana and LSD to get beyond the TV scenario? To enhance creativity? As catalysts to deepen wisdom?

If so, you will be helped by making explicit the religious nature of your psychedelic activities. To give meaning to your own script, to clarify your relationships with others, and to cope with the present legal set-up, you will do well to start your own religion.

How to Start Your Own Religion

First, decide with whom you will make the voyage of discovery. If you have a family, certainly you will include them. If you have close friends, you will certainly want to include them. The question, with whom do I league for spiritual discovery? is a fascinating exercise.

Next, sit down with your spiritual companions and put on a page the plan for your trip. Write down and define your:

Goals

Roles

Rituals

Rules

Vocabulary

Values

Space-time locales

Mythic context

Here is an interesting exercise. You will learn a lot about yourself and your companions. You will see where you are and where you are not.

You will find it necessary to be explicit about the way your clan handles authority, responsibility, sexual relations, money, economics, defense, communication.

In short, you are forming not only your own religion but your own natural political unit. This is inevitable because the basic political unit is exactly the same as the basic spiritual grouping – the clan. Did you really believe that church was only where you went for an hour on Sunday morning?

Make your clan unique. Do not slavishly copy the roles and language of other groups. The beauty of cellular life is that each unit is both so incredibly complexly similar and also so unique. The more you understand the infinite complexity of life, the more you treasure both the similarities and the differences. But you have to be turned on to see it. At the level of the studio-prop game, both the similarities and the differences are trivial.

In defining the goal of your religion, you need not use conventional religious language. You don't have to make your spiritual journey sound 'religious'. Religion cannot be pompous and high-flown. Religion is consciousness expansion, centered in the body and defined exactly the way it sounds best to you. Don't be intimidated by Caesar's Hollywood fake versions of religiosity. If life has a meaning for you beyond the TV-studio game, you are religious. Spell it out.

So write out your own language for the trip: *God* or *evolution, acid* or *sacrament, guide* or *guru, purgatorial redemption* or *bad trip, mystic revelation* or *good high.* Say it naturally.

Develop your own rituals and costumes. Robes or gray flannel suits, amulets or tattoos. You will eventually find yourself engaged in a series of sacred moments which feel right to you.

Step by step

    all your actions

        will take on a sacra

           mental meaning. Inevit

             ably you will create a ritual

                sequence for each sense organ

                    and for each of the basic energy ex

                        changes – eating, bathing, mating, etc.

You must be explicit about the space-time arrangement for your God game. Each room in your home will contain a shrine. Your house will not be a TV actor's dressing room but rather a spiritual center. Regular rhythms of worship will emerge – daily meditation (turn-on) sessions (with or without marijuana), and once a week or once a month you will devote a whole day to turning on. Time your worship to the rhythm of the seasons, to the planetary calendar.

Spell out on paper explicit plan$ for handling financial interaction$. Money i$ a completely irrational focu$ for mo$t We$terner$. A$ $oon a$ your clan member$ detach them$elve$ emotionally from money, you will discover how easy it is to survive economically. There must be a complete and collaborative pooling of money and work energy. Any $elfi$h holding back of dollar$ or muscular energy will weaken the clan. Each clan, as it drops out of the American game, must appraise its resources and figure out how to barter with other groups. Each clan will develop its own productivity.

Sexuality is the downfall of most religious cults. Clarity and honesty are necessary. Karmic accidental differences exist in people's sexual makeup. Basically, each man is made to mate with one woman. Heterosexual monogamous fidelity is the only natural way of sexual union. However, because this is the Kali Yuga, and because we live in the final stages of a sick society, sexual variations are inevitable.

Your mode of sexual union is the key to your religion. You cannot escape this. The way you ball (or avoid balling) is your central sacramental activity. The sexual proclivity of the clan must be explicit and inflexible. Do not attempt to establish clan relationships with persons of a different sexual persuasion. There is no value judgment here. Sex is sacred. People of like sexual temperament must form their own spiritual cults. Homosexuality is not an illness. It is a religious way of life. Homosexuals should accept their state as a religious path. Homosexuals cannot join heterosexual clans. Homosexuals should treasure, glorify, their own sexual yoga. Their right to pursue their sacred bodily yoga is guaranteed to them. Heterosexual clans can support, help, learn from, teach homosexual clans, but the difference must be preserved – with mutual respect.

Some spiritual people are not compatible with the monogamous union and prefer a freer sexual regime, the group marriage. Good! Many tribes and clans throughout the planet have flourished in complete and holy promiscuity. But be explicit. Painful confusions occur if sexual orientations and sexual taboos (cellular and physical, not psychological or cultural) are disregarded in forming clans.

Select clan members who share or complement your style, your way of tuning in, your temperament, your sexual orientation.

The aim of clan living is to subordinate the ego game to the family game – the clan game.

You will do well to have an explicit connection to a mythic figure. You must select a historical psychedelic guide. You must know your mythic origins. Facts and news are reports from the current TV drama. They have no relevance to your 2-billion-year-old divinity. Myth is the report from the cellular memory bank. Myths humanize the recurrent themes of evolution.

You select a myth as a reminder that you are part of an ancient and holy process. You select a myth to guide you when you drop out of the narrow confines of the fake-prop studio set.

Your mythic guide must be one who has solved the death-rebirth riddle. A TV drama hero cannot help you. Caesar, Napoleon, Kennedy are no help to your cellular orientation. Christ, Lao-tse, Hermes Trismegistus, Socrates are recurrent turn-on figures.

You will find it absolutely necessary to leave the city. Urban living is spiritually suicidal. The cities of America are about to crumble as did Rome and Babylon. Go to the land. Go to the sea.

Psychedelic centers located in cities will serve as collecting areas. Thousands of spiritual seekers are coming to urban districts where they meet in meditation centers and psychedelic assembly places. There they form their clans. They migrate from the city. [...]

Unless you form your own new religion and devote an increasing amount of your energies to it, you are (however exciting your personality TV role) a robot. Your new religion can be formed only by you. Do not wait for a messiah. Do it yourself. Now.

C7 Joan Harrison, A testament

From D. Hunt (1980) *The Cult Explosion*, Eugene, Oregon, Harvest House, pp.10, 11.

I was a seeker looking for ultimate answers. My search began ... in psychoanalysis ... encounter groups and ... psychedelic drugs.

I was particularly impressed by Timothy Leary's book *The Psychedelic Experience*, which showed the relationship between LSD and mystical experiences of Tibetan Buddhist monks. That led me into Eastern mysticism.

I became interested in TM in 1967. It was very big in Berkeley, and many of my friends were getting into it. There were posters all over town advertising TM as a way to bliss consciousness, relaxation, and one's full potential.

I was looking for ... answers to life. That was the main reason why I got into TM. And I did experience superficial results right away – relaxation and a euphoric feeling that would come and go. [...]

I became a TM teacher and had many supernatural experiences. Definitely it wasn't just in my mind, because I didn't even believe such things were possible until I experienced them. [...]

For those who really got into it, TM was like taking a rocket ship into another state of consciousness where their whole view of reality and of God would be changed.

C8 David Berg, 'Who are the rebels?'

From Deborah (Linda Berg) Davis with Bill Davis (1984) *The Children of God: The Inside Story*, Grand Rapids, Mich., Zondervan, citing the 'Mo Letter E' written by David Berg in the late Sixties, pp.38, 39, footnotes omitted.

So you say the youth of today are rebels – rebellious, defiant, lawbreakers and seeking to destroy society. But really, who are the rebels? We, or you, our parents? ...

The kids are rebellious against society because the society is anti-God. Everything the kids are – the way they look, the way they act – in a large degree it's a rebellion against the pattern of society, but it's a return actually to the Lord's pattern.

How can they [the youth] rebel against God's laws? How can they rebel against His Word? – They don't know it. But their parents did and they rebelled just like the Children of Israel. The parents were the rebels. Only the children were allowed in the Promised Land. [...]

The parents want them to follow in their footsteps in a selfish dog-eat-dog economy in which they not only murder one another, but they conduct massive slaughters of whole nations. ... The young people are sick and fed up with what really amounts to a pagan, cruel, whoremongering, false Christianity. They're trying to return to the peace-loving religions of old, including ancient Christianity, and the parents will have none of it.

So who are the rebels? If you mean rebels against ... the looks of the ancients and the economy of the ancients, then the parents are the rebels.

But if you mean rebels against this recent modern plastic, artificial man-made, gadget-filled, money crazy, whoremongering, sex-mad, religiously hypocritical society of the parents of today, yes, we the youth of today are rebels and revolutionists. ... We want to return to the patterns of Noah and Abraham and Moses and the judges and kings, like David and Solomon, and the prophets of old – indeed the pattern of Jesus Christ Himself and His disciples and the martyrs of the Church.

Who are the real rebels of today? ... We are the true lovers of peace and love and truth and beauty and God and freedom: whereas you, our parents, are the most God-defying, commandment-breaking, insanely rebellious rebels of all time, who are on the brink of destroying and polluting all of us and our world if we do not rise up against you in the name of God and try to stop you.

C9   James Nolan, 'Jesus now: hogwash and holy water'

From J. Nolan (1971) 'Jesus now: hogwash and holy water', *Ramparts*, August, pp.20–26.

Swept along in the squall of *Peace on Right Now You-Name-It Against The War* placards at the Spring Offensive in San Francisco waved a flimsy blue poster with drippy red lettering that read *Jesus: A Bridge Over Troubled Waters*. The bearer wasn't a collared cleric or a Youth Fellowshipper chalking up merit points for heaven, but a scroungy, ponchoed, bell-bottomed veteran of the streets. Anyone at all familiar with what is happening in California simply nodded a recognition – ah, a Jesus freak – accepted his tract and plowed on to the polo field. A few stopped and stared, obviously shaken to their Sunday School roots by the very idea of freak evangelism, a fairly new breed in the hip-liberation menagerie. But there he was, marching right-on along with the red armbands, the lavender headbands, the brown berets, the black berets, the inverted flags, the hardstepping women, the saffron robes and the green earth insignias. And this barefoot boy with his flimsy blue bridge-over-troubled-waters certainly did not seem to have come at the wrong time or to the wrong place with whatever message he had to give America in the Seventies.

The message of Jesus-freaks, in case you haven't been able to skim their tracts or sit still through their spiel, is simply down-home, Jesus-is-the-way, evangelical fundamentalism delivered with flower-child innocence and visionary fervor. The movement is incredibly broad-based. There are over 200 Jesus communes in California alone, a Jesus headquarters coffeehouse or headshop in every major city in the country, and missionary troops in motion everywhere, converting, founding, funding and then moving on. The large wall map at the Christian World Liberation Front in Berkeley is studded with pinheads marking the places where the movement has taken root, giving you the same they're-really-out-there feeling of a Howard Johnson's placemat map. Despite the bare feet and patches, it really is big time stuff, concentrated mostly along the West Coast in Vancouver, Seattle, the Bay Area and Los Angeles, with another contingent distributed throughout the South. Most Jesus communes publish amateurish underground newspapers and bear names like the folksy Children of God Soul Clinic, the obscure Koinonia Community, and the clever House of the Risen Son.

American blow-your-mind, zappo-revolutionary kids are literally flocking into these fundamentalist conversion parlors and coming out with handfuls of psychedelic-looking tracts, a 'Biblical' set of morals and big Billy James Hargis friend-do-you-know-the-Lord grins. The Jesus houses offer a place to crash indefinitely, free food and free medical care, a toothbrush and comb, enough to do and more than enough to believe in;

and there's usually a Mother or Daddy figure who, despite the preaching and soul-saving, really seems to care, and won't make you cut your hair. All in all, it's an unbeatable combination if you're 18 years old, a runaway from some cowtown Paducah or plastic Executive Oaks, used to dropping acid by the six-pack, alone and penniless in the ghetto-zoo, fucked-up and fucked-over, testing around for some ultimate reality trip, with nothing to do and no place in particular to do it.

The Jesus trip is particularly attractive to children brought up in staunchly religious homes (there are many former Catholics and Baptists) or to kids reared on suburban textbook agnosticism, the ones who are lost even before they've found anything to be lost from. Most of the converted are between 14 and 20, and they possess an amazingly glowing energy and commitment, all shining as though they've just washed their hair. Maybe the Jesus movement is only a later version of Love-Generation-Haight-Ashbury optimism, the flowers-and-transcendence stage of growing up American, that will eventually turn the same worn path to skepticism and militancy when they reach 23.

But it can't be this alone. There is a great difference between an imported novelty fetish like, say, Hare Krishna – which is essentially hip faddism in search of faith, a turn-on that soon burns itself out into a religion of Indian-print bedspreads and incense, and deeply ingrained, evangelical Christianity – upon which, they tell us, this Nation of Ours was founded and the West was Won. They are partially right, of course. And, even if Jesus was not in cahoots with Christopher Columbus and Kit Carson, Bible Belt Christianity is not simply another American fad – it runs too deep in too many people. Like that trout-fishing cabin in Utah, it is at least what part of America is all about. Whether the new masses of Jesus-freaks are only visiting or whether they plan to stay, they are pitching their tents very close to one of the main arteries of the American heart.

Jesus-freaks have introduced only a few real variations to Bible-pounding, tent-revival, fundamentalist Christianity, among them street language (Jesus is no longer Lord and Savior but Leader and Liberator) and the communal lifestyle. But over-arching all else is a passionate belief that the world will end within their lifetime while Jesus returns to rapture them off to a very literal heaven with streets of gold and angels twanging on electric-amp harps, the thought of which clouds their eyes and leaves them murmuring 'fa-a-ar out'.

Fundamentalists are a tricky lot. Between the ages of 6 and 12 I probably gave my life to Christ about two or three hundred times in the fundamentalist church in New Orleans that I was combed and bow-tied off to every Sunday morning. *Are you washed in the blood of the lamb? Do you recognize yourself as a miserable sinner wretched in God's sight? Are you ready to get down on your knees and accept Jesus into your heart as your own personal savior? All those ready to make a decision for Christ, just step on up to the front of the church and praise* deedum

deedum deedee. Sunday morning was bringing in the sheaves (and usually the same old ones), followed by the Sunday evening Saved for Christ Scoreboard, followed by Bible study with Dixie cups of punch and cookies, everyone feverishly fanning himself in the sultry New Orleans night with picture fans of Jesus-in-the-Garden-of-Gethsemane supplied by a local mortuary. It was a hell of a way to grow up, I suppose, but I eventually felt secure enough in my solid-rock salvation to sneak off to the drugstore from Bible study to read *Playboy*, though not without the puffy red face of the preacher following me in my mind, exhorting me to give my life to Christ again.

The fundamentalist works on an appeal to guilt, which suburban drop-outs are particularly full of, on a thundering fear of hell and a candy-sweet promise of heaven, on a complete negation of any other possible means to happiness, and on a repetition of phrases so unrelenting as to make a Madison Avenue advertiser stutter. You either give in or walk out. His pitch is an express train with only one stop: your salvation. All questions are answered by vague and enigmatic Bible quotations followed by chapter and verse number so that you cannot *possibly* doubt their truth, and key simplicities are underlined in verbal red. If you protest even the slightest, you are told that Satan has planted his seed in your brain, a notion with disturbing implications to be sure, and, if you protest too much, you are told that you are possessed of a demon from which only the blood of Jesus Christ can deliver you. Then it starts all over again, back to original sin and the goddamned Garden of Eden. In the end, if you become a passive enough listener, you are rewarded with a paperback Bible, the converter tape-loop is shut-off, pleasantries are exchanged about automobiles or summer vacations, and you can leave, promising to read the Bible and 'look over' the tract.

I o.d.'d on peanut butter when I was 10 and fundamentalism when I was 12 and haven't been able to stand the taste of either since. Every time I hear the familiar strains of one of those mournful old hymns, I gag on years of undigested punch and cookies. I can make no pretense about my feelings about fundamentalist theology, fundamentalist evangelism and the whole fundamentalist fandango of faith-healing, Bible-beating and tent-shouting: it's hogwash. It is a political opiate and a psychological crutch. Fundamentalism is truly the wading pool of religious faith, reserved for the fearful, the guilt-ridden and the childish, for those unprepared to dive, to make their faith leap into a political reality or mystical depth. [...]

Sitting around the nicely table-clothed, properly-set dinner table at Harvest House 'commune' in San Francisco, brought an incredible psychological flashback to my punch-and-cookie years in Youth Fellowship. The feeling was amazingly the same, a sort of strained institutional good humor. Pass the biscuits and praise the Lord. Talking with the soft-spoken, Alabama-bred Oliver Heath, an ordained minister of the Southern Baptist Church and graduate of the Golden Gate

Theological Seminary in Marin County, a fundamentalist school which is the seedbed of the Jesus movement in northern California, while his Louisiana-bred wife, Mary Louise, padded about in fluffy pink bedroom slippers and curlers serving up cornbread and potluck, it really felt like a corner of Kansas pocketed by comic mistakes in the teeming heavy freak scene of Haight-Ashbury.

A shaggy young hippie-type in a corner was for some reason knotted into a red tie and starched white collar with an ill-fitting grey sport-coat, and kept giving me that strangled home-for-the-holidays look which I remember only too well. He looked as though he were trying to win the keys to the family car for the night by painfully selfconscious good behavior. Oliver kept interrupting our discussion of original sin and repentance to deliver stern reprimands to various scruffies: 'Eric, you know you're not allowed to smoke in here, put that cigarette out!' and 'Dennis, don't you have a comb!' Eric, the communal scapegoat, at 17 is so disoriented by his 100 or more acid trips that he would bring back groceries to the wrong apartment door, and therefore, the others explained, could not be trusted, so everyone prayed constantly for his soul to be purged of its demons. And Dennis was having Satan's seed planted in his brain by such Little Rascals' naughties as not coming home right after school but sneaking off to some suspicious Haight hash house, where he brushed shoulders with the devil's crowd, all fanged and horned and high on the Killer Weed.

At Harvest House there was much talk of the Enemy, who was on guard at all times, waiting for any opportunity to slither into their midst like some green gaseous malevolence sent from below. A young girl named Rose Marie, who seemed to become upset often, pleaded to the others that she needed to be left alone when she was disturbed, but the others insisted that such was the easiest time for Satan to stick a lie into her head. *The devil gonna git your soul, honey.* Huddling like a small child in a large, overstuffed armchair, Rose Marie seemed close to freaking out.

Like a camp shower room, all the towels in the bathroom were pegged and labeled *Mary, Johnny, Sue* and so forth; and for some reason that simpy Sunday School picture of Jesus-in-the-Garden-of-Gethsemane was iconed over the toothbrush rack, probably to remind early morning brushers of their oft-bannered slogan: *after Jesus, everything else is toothpaste.* The orderly atmosphere, I was informed, was enforced in order to keep the 'children' together – but not too together, for according to the strict precepts of Biblical morality (no screwing without a license), the boys and girls are carefully chaperoned and sleep in segregated quarters because 'too much friction between the sexes tends to distract from the Lord's work'.

The Lord's work at Harvest House consists of putting out a Jesus newspaper called the *Oracle* (which is an almost campy, religious, calendar-art revival of the old Haight-Ashbury *Oracle*), running a free store, printing tracts, helping to manage three adjoining communes in the city, and evangelizing in the streets. After Bible study at a local church that evening, the commune regathered for a sort of community encounter with each other. One wide-eyed young man confessed that, when he thought of all the things he had done wrong that very day, it was like going up and hitting God right in the mouth, WHAMMM. A very pregnant girl offered that, since she had become a Christian, she couldn't associate with her friends – they are 'so steeped in sin', as she had been. Oliver told the group: 'If you think I'm a phony, if you think I'm dishonest, if you think I'm not like Jesus, tell me now.' Everyone beamed. A 17 year old volunteered that he now felt closer to his parents (since he accepted Jesus) than ever before, and that his father had taught him not to lie and, even after all the acid and all the meth, that still made sense.

Spontaneous eruptions of conscience continued for about an hour, moving around the room like some T-group rendition of the White Tornado. My heart sank. Here it all was – the entire American mythology of growing up, freaking out, and running away; the well-powdered, Bible-preaching forces of Aunt Em, Aunt Sally, Miss Crabtree, confronting the primitive scraggly-haired, dirty faces of the perverse, freedom-loving Dorothy, Huck Finn and Our Gang; and Aunt Sally was winning. Dorothy had finally made it back to hug her Aunt Em and gasp about the bad dreams she had just tripped through. The high school drop-outs in the room were all going back to school, the rest were getting jobs and re-establishing contact with their parents or going home. Intuitively I realized what the Jesus trip really meant to a lot of these kids; it is a way of getting back to Kansas from the tortured and confusing psychedelic world of surreal low-life munchkins, witches and wizards, back to the comfort and reassurance of your own backyard. Back from the drop-a-tab, crashpad spirituality of cross-country hitching, of protesting and confronting, of open-ended grooving that somehow always ended with the needle, getting busted, having your head swagger-sticked open, or getting pregnant. I didn't, I couldn't, have any more questions of these people.

I still think Aunt Sally with her comb and her toothbrush and her Bible is a stifling bitch, but I know those dead-ends that the river can lead to, and that sometimes you have to try to get back to where you once belonged. This, Oliver explained to me, is the function of Harvest House and others like it: it is a hospital, a half-way house back to stability and wholeness through, he added, Jesus Christ. There is a time to argue theology, and I think his is wrong. There is a time to argue politics, and I think, whether he knows it or not, his are reactionary. There is a time to argue the revolution, and the Jesus-movement is definitely *not* where it's happening. But there is also a time to shut up and let people heal. And this, if Harvest House can accomplish it, may be worth all the rest. [...]

As to the financial source of all these free newspapers, free pass-outs, free food and lodging, the Jesus people respond with big lilies-of-the-field smiles: the Lord Provideth. And the Lord worketh in some pretty mysterious ways, they'll say, reeling out stories of $10 bills wrapped in toilet paper sent in the mail every month, commune members' back paychecks arriving miraculously on rent day as the landlord menacingly twirls his moustache, $50 for car payments sent from churches back home in Alabama. Despite their patches-and-leftovers life style, Jesus people usually have an impressive business set-up. One example is Harvest House which, together with Zion's Inn, a Jesus commune in nearby Marin County, have formed the Solid Rock Construction Company, which does housepainting. Most of the communes have prospered because of a Calvinist dedication to hard work and self-improvement, making carpenters, printers and soup-makers of the aimless kids who stumble in. The kids seem to enjoy the work, bustling about with sacks of flour and bundles of paper with a door-to-door-for McCarthy cheerfulness. After all, with no dope or sex or Zap Comix or TV, what else is there to do?

Suddenly, Jesus is everywhere. Jesus buttons, Jesus sweatshirts. Honk-if-you-love-Jesus bumper-stickers, Jesus day-glo posters, Jesus on the cover of the *Whole Earth Supplement*, Jesus comics, the Jesus look, *Jesus Christ, Superstar*, Jesus rock.

Jesus is even more popular than John Lennon. Put your hand in the hand of the man from Galilee, how I changed from Krishna to Christ, how I lost 300 lbs. and saved my marriage with Jesus. Somehow fundamentalist evangelism has caught up with mass media and is plastering stickers, converting rock stars and plugging in amps all over the place.

As people lose their grip on the revolution, they seem to be grasping for absolutes. In the heavily moralistic South, the Jesus line seems appropriate – else no one would listen. But in the super-relativistic do-your-own-thing, mobile California scene, it is jarring. Yet it is perhaps this absolutism which attracts the blown-out 17 year old who simply has nothing to do. High school has not prepared him for anything creative or constructive; it has only driven him to drop acid three times a week. Once that's done, it is impossible to be processed through the mind-cannery of a large university for very long. Nor can he go back home to the carport and a bag-boy job in the supermarket. With neither answers nor alternatives, with the visionary acid world of angels and demons his only certainty, the fast talking, self-confident preacher steps in and puts his big Biblical foot down, taps it in a few familiar rhythms, stamps it in the fervor of his belief and everything falls into place.

The real issue at stake here is that drug-blown, pop-freaked, ego-defenseless kids, who in their innocence, openness and idealism are truly beautiful, can easily become the victims of a desperate evangelism of any kind – that, just as a handful of Hell's Angels can stomp in and take over a pop festival, a small collection of bell-bottomed Baptists and, at worst, Elmer Gantrys, can begin to redirect whole generations into their scripture-lined tents. It is the same with the Scientologists, the chanters, the T-groupies, the occultists and certain of the liberationist bandwagons.

The preacher does not offer a choice between a confusing array of life styles and locations, but rather a choice between eternal salvation and eternal damnation – which isn't a choice at all. Whether the content of his message is hogwash or holy water doesn't make too much difference. Whether these evangelistic Christians are, as Nietzsche accused, predatory birds who swoop down on weak life in distress or, in a more charitable view, fanatical do-gooders with an overly developed, paternal sense, makes little difference. The fact is, these people, and the leaders of other mass movements like them, are bringing freaked-out kids down and placing them in a community situation where roles are assigned and talents encouraged.

Mything-out on Jesus, though, is not too different from spacing-out on drugs; and once Jesus has brought them down from drugs, what's going to bring them down from Jesus? This kind of ultimate-trip carousel will continue to spin as long as, America being what it is now, there is nothing to come down to. So finally, a message to Jesus-boppers: If your apocalypse does not happen on schedule, and if and when you are lemming off in some new direction, realizing the torment and difficulty of true sainthood and that salvation is not just a shot of anything away, spare us one vision: a littered, trampled post-festival shambles with Jesus Christ, a blown-out superstar, back where he started, unplugging the amps and picking up the empty dixie punch cups and sweeping up the cookie crumbs scattered by the marauding packs of crowded, lonely people: no one was saved.

C10 Anonymous letter

From R. Enroth (1977, British edn) *Youth Brainwashing, and the Extremist Cults*, Exeter, Paternoster Press, first published in 1977, Grand Rapids, Mich., Zondervan.

Dear Mom and Dad.

I don't know if you know that I have left [name of midwestern city]. But the Lord led two Christian brothers to town, and I feel the Lord led me to go with them and serve the Lord, leaving all material possessions I had, except for what I needed. We have gathered with the others in the Lord, and it was good to meet the sisters in the church. We go by no name, but we are Christians living the way the Bible teaches, clinging only to the Lord.

We dress modestly as the Lord teaches – the women in long skirts and smocks and the men in long robes – hand-sewn by the women. The Lord provides us with food.

We travel all over to speak to souls about the Lord. I have found a real peace, nothing like I could find living in the world.

I have read and read in the King James Version of the Scriptures and just have not found a reason to come back and live a life serving man or going to school to get some degree of carnal knowledge. I always thought that God was leading me to work at the dentist's office and leading me to go to beauty school. But His will is that we *live for Him* and tell others of Him. That is my purpose now, and I pray God will give you grace not to worry about me.

It's really a blessing to live separated from the way of the world. I'm sure you have a lot of questions and many people don't understand how we can actually live by faith and take no thought of what we will eat or drink or wear tomorrow. But I haven't gone hungry or been unclothed yet. We've found the world to be very wasteful. Grocery stores that throw out good food – still packaged, sometimes cold milk, yoghurt and cottage cheese, much fruit and vegetables and bread, donuts ... it's truly amazing. We have also been out in the wilderness and the Lord has provided – so we don't depend on these stores. We depend on the Creator!

I just don't feel I can or should explain everything to you. I just pray that the Lord will start to open your eyes to the way the world is falling. Christians need to get out of it. Praise God. There is a lot of persecution to endure, but the Lord's always faithful if we're true to Him. When I was living in the world I kept thinking that there's got to be a way to live by faith and do as the Word says. But I never thought it was possible until I stepped out on a limb and left with those two brothers who were passing through town. When I saw them, I thought they looked like disciples, or how I had visioned disciples in the Bible – robes, sandals, beards. I found they were really following the Bible. I have had the Bible pounded into me all my life and never really understood how it could apply to my life until now. Praise God.

I've found that when one is living according to the Scriptures and not the laws of this world or the tradition of men, persecution is here. We've had some thrown in jail for serving the Lord, some put in mental institutions, accused of being insane, and some set down in front of psychiatrists to try and get this brainwashed way of life out of them. We've had many lies told about us and you may have even heard some on TV. It's very sad to this soul, because so many are rejecting God in persecuting us.

I pray that this letter makes sense to you; I write with much hope that you'll understand. I know it must be hard, because you miss this flesh of your daughter, but I hope you begin to realise that this flesh will pass away and this soul will live forever. I'm just doing what I feel is right for this soul.

I pray that I have not preached in this letter, as it doesn't seem to be the woman's place. I only want you to have a good understanding of what

I'm doing, as we've seen many parents deceived and really fight God's work in a life.

I know you miss me and my flesh, and with the worldly holidays coming up I'll probably be missed more. But it's all going to make sense to me on judgment day – praise God. Those celebrations, those gifts are going to mean nothing, and though this flesh is lustful and wants riches on this earth, the soul is blessed to leave it behind. I don't know what happened with the stuff I owned back there. It can be sold or thrown out as far as I care – or given away. I didn't want it to be a burden for people, but when I saw the light I just had to leave before Satan confused me and snared me to stay in the comforts of the flesh.

I will call or see you when the Lord leads me to.

As He leads.
I'm in His care

C11 'The Jesus revolution'

From *Time* magazine, 21 June 1971, pp.56, 59–63.

The New Rebel Cry: Jesus Is Coming!

WANTED

JESUS CHRIST

**ALIAS: THE MESSIAH, THE SON OF
GOD, KING OF KINGS, LORD OF
LORDS, PRINCE OF PEACE, ETC.**

▶ Notorious leader of an underground liberation movement

▶ Wanted for the following charges:
 – Practicing medicine, winemaking and food distribution without a license.
 – Interfering with businessmen in the temple.
 – Associating with known criminals, radicals, subversives, prostitutes and street people.
 – Claiming to have the authority to make people into God's children.

APPEARANCE: Typical hippie type – long hair, beard, robe, sandals.

▶ Hangs around slum areas, few rich friends, often sneaks out into the desert.

BEWARE: This man is extremely dangerous. His insidiously inflammatory message is particularly dangerous to young people who haven't been taught to ignore him yet. He changes men and claims to set them free.

WARNING: HE IS STILL AT LARGE!

He is indeed. As the words of this Wanted poster from a Christian underground newspaper demonstrate, Jesus is alive and well and living in the radical spiritual fervor of a growing number of young Americans who have proclaimed an extraordinary religious revolution in his name. Their message: the Bible is true, miracles happen, God really did so love the world that he gave it his only begotten son. In 1966 Beatle John Lennon casually remarked that the Beatles were more popular than Jesus Christ: now the Beatles are shattered, and George Harrison is singing *My Sweet Lord*. The new young followers of Jesus listen to Harrison, but they turn on only to the words of their Master: 'For where two or three are gathered together in my name, there am I in the midst of them.'

It is a startling development for a generation that has been constantly accused of tripping out or copping out with sex, drugs and violence. Now, embracing the most persistent symbol of purity, selflessness and brotherly love in the history of Western man, they are afire with a Pentecostal passion for sharing their new vision with others. Freshfaced, wide-eyed young girls and earnest young men badger businessmen and shoppers on Hollywood Boulevard, near the Lincoln Memorial, in Dallas, in Detroit and in Wichita, 'witnessing' for Christ with breathless exhortations. Christian coffeehouses have opened in many cities, signaling their faith even in their names: The Way Word in Greenwich Village, the Catacombs in Seattle, I Am in Spokane. A strip joint has been converted to a 'Christian nightclub' in San Antonio. Communal 'Christian houses' are multiplying like loaves and fishes for youngsters hungry for homes, many reaching out to the troubled with round-the-clock telephone hot lines. Bibles abound: whether the cherished, fur-covered King James Version or scruffy, back-pocket paperbacks, they are invariably well-thumbed and often memorized. 'It's like a glacier,' says 'Jesus-Rock' Singer Larry Norman, 24, 'it's growing and there's no stopping it.'

There is an uncommon morning freshness to this movement, a buoyant atmosphere of hope and love along with the usual rebel zeal. Some converts seem to enjoy translating their new faith into everyday life, like those who answer the phone with 'Jesus loves you' instead of 'hello'. But their love seems more sincere than a slogan, deeper than the fast-fading sentiments of the flower children; what startles the outsider is the extraordinary sense of joy that they are able to communicate. Of course, as in any fresh religious movement, zealotry is never far away. Some in the movement even have divine timetables. Says Founder Bill Bright of the Campus Crusade for Christ: 'Our target date for saturating the US with the gospel of Jesus Christ is 1976 – and the world by 1980. Of course, if the Lord wants to work a bit slower, that's OK.'

Some of the fascination for Jesus among the young may simply be belated hero worship of a fellow rebel, the first great martyr to the cause of peace and brotherhood. Not so, however, for the vast majority in the Jesus movement. If any one mark clearly identifies them it is their total belief in an awesome, supernatural Jesus Christ, not just a marvelous man who lived 2,000 years ago but a living God who is both Saviour and Judge, the ruler of their destinies. Their lives revolve around the necessity for an intense personal relationship with that Jesus, and the belief that such a relationship should condition every human life. They act as if divine intervention guides their every movement and can be counted on to solve every problem. Many of them have had serious personal difficulties before their conversions; a good portion of the movement is really a May–December marriage of conservative religion and the rebellious counterculture, and many of the converts have come to Christ from the fraudulent promises of drugs. Now they subscribe strictly to the Ten Commandments, rather than to the situation ethics of the 'new morality' – although, like St Paul, they are often tolerant of old failings among new converts.

The Jesus revolution rejects not only the material values of conventional America but the prevailing wisdom of American theology. Success often means an impersonal and despiritualized life that increasingly finds release in sexploration, status, alcohol and conspicuous consumption. Christianity – or at least the brand of it preached in prestige seminaries, pulpits and church offices over recent decades – has emphasized an immanent God of nature and social movement, not the new movement's transcendental, personal God who comes to earth in the person of Jesus, in the lives of individuals, in miracles [original text referred here to boxed article 'Many things to many men', now reproduced on p.00]. The Jesus revolution, in short, is one that denies the virtues of the Secular City and heaps scorn on the message that God was ever dead. Why?

But why not? This is the generation that has burned out many of its lights and lives before it is old enough to vote. 'The first thing I realized was how different it is to go to high school today', wrote Maureen Orth in a 'Last Supplement' to the *Whole Earth Catalog*. 'Acid trips in the seventh grade, sex in the eighth, the Viet Nam War a daily serial on TV since you were nine, parents and school worse than 'irrelevant' – meaningless. No wonder Jesus is making a great comeback.' The death of authority brought the curse of uncertainty. As Thomas Farber writes in *Tales for the Son of My Unborn Child*: 'The freedom from work, from restraint, from accountability, wondrous in its inception, became banal and counterfeit. Without rules there was no way to say no, and worse, no way to say yes.'

The search for a 'yes' led thousands to the Oriental and the mystical, the occult and even Satanism before they drew once again on familiar roots. One of the nation's successful young evangelists, Richard Hoag, 24, believes that many of his youthful converts see Jesus as a marvelous father figure. 'The kids are searching for authority, love and understanding – ingredients missing at home. Jesus is what their fathers aren't.' Adds Baptist Pastor John Bisagno: 'I'm amazed at how many people I've counseled who have never heard their fathers say "I love you".'

Christ Couture

The enthusiasm is not universal. By no means a majority of the young, or their elders, are soldiers in the revolution – any more than they were flower children or acid trippers. Some call the Jesus movement a fad or just another bad trip. Is it? Is the growing fascination with Jesus a passing, adolescent infatuation? There are obvious fad aspects: Jesus shirts (JESUS IS MY LORD) bumper stickers (SMILE, GOD LOVES YOU), posters, buttons (THE MESSIAH IS THE MESSAGE) and, inevitably, a Jesus-People wristwatch. Some followers are affecting a Christ couture: white pants and tunics, Mexican-peasant style. There are *de rigueur* catch phrases: endless 'Praise Gods' and 'Bless Yous'. There is even a 'Jesus cheer' – 'Give me a J, give me an E ...' Rapidly catching on is the Jesus-People 'sign', a raised arm with clenched fist, the index finger pointed heavenward, to indicate Jesus as the 'one way' to salvation. 'If it is a fad,' says Evangelist Billy Graham, 'I welcome it.'

There are signs that the movement is something quite a bit larger than a theological Hula-Hoop, something more lasting than a religious Woodstock. It cuts across nearly all the social dividing lines, from crew cut to long hair, right to left, rich to poor. It shows considerable staying power: many who were in its faint beginnings in 1967 are still leading it. It has been powerful enough to divert many young people from serious drug addiction. Its appeal is ecumenical, attracting Roman Catholics and Jews, Protestants of every persuasion and many with no religion at all. Catholics visit Protestant churches with a new empathy, and Protestants find themselves chatting with nuns and openly enjoying Mass. 'We are all brothers in the body of Christ', says a California Catholic lay leader, and he adds: 'We are on the threshold of the greatest spiritual revival the US has ever experienced.'

Pentecostals and Millenarians

Spiritual revivals are, of course, a longstanding American tradition. George Whitefield and Jonathan Edwards led the first Great Awakening in the 1740s and there have been others since: the frontier camp meetings at the beginning of the 19th century, the great revival of the 1850s, and the Pentecostal explosion at the beginning of the 20th century. The Jesus revolution, like the others, has a flavor peculiarly American. Its strong Pentecostalism emphasizes such esoteric spiritual gifts as speaking in tongues and healing by faith. For many, there exists a firm conviction that Jesus' Second Coming is literally at hand. Proclaiming the imminent end of the world and Last Judgment like so many dread guards, some millenarians chart the signs of the Apocalypse with the aid of handbooks like *The Late Great Planet Earth*. They see smog and pollution prophesied in *Isaiah*; the taking of Old Jerusalem by the Jews, and the admission of ten nations into the Common Market as signs that the end is near.

The movement is apart from, rather than against, established religion; converts often speak disparagingly of the blandness or hypocrisy of their former churches, but others work comfortably as a supplementary, revitalizing force of change from within. The movement, in fact, is one of considerable flexibility and vitality, drawing from three vigorous spiritual streams that, despite differences in dress, manner and theology, effectively reinforce one another.

THE JESUS PEOPLE, also known as Street Christians or Jesus Freaks, are the most visible; it is they who have blended the counterculture and conservative religion. Many trace their beginnings to the 1967 flower era in San Francisco, but there were almost simultaneous stirrings in other areas. Some, but by no means all, affect the hippie style, others have forsworn it as part of their new lives.

THE STRAIGHT PEOPLE, by far the largest group, are mainly active in interdenominational, evangelical campus and youth movements. Once merely an arm of evangelical Protestantism, they are now more ecumenical – a force almost independent of the churches that spawned them. Most of them are Middle America, campus types: neatly coiffed hair and Sears, Roebuck clothes styles.

THE CATHOLIC PENTECOSTALS, like the Jesus People, emerged unexpectedly and dramatically in 1967. Publicly austere but privately ecstatic in their devotion to the Holy Spirit, they remain loyal to the church but unsettle some in the hierarchy. In a sense they are following the lead of mainstream Protestant Neo-Pentecostals, who have been leading charismatic renewal movements in their own churches for a decade.

Together, all three movements may number in the hundreds of thousands nationally, conceivably many more, but any figure is a guess. The Catholic Pentecostals, often meeting in the privacy of members' homes, may number 10,000, but some observers believe that they could easily be three times that. Those converted by the straight evangelicals generally wind up on established church rolls, but are likely to be in the hundreds of thousands; the evangelistic staffs alone account for more than 5,000 people. The Jesus People – surely many thousands – are the most difficult to count. They often cluster in communes or, as they prefer to call them, 'Christian houses'; the Rev. Edward Plowman, historian of the movement, estimates that there are 600 across the US. There is no doubt about their growth: Evangelist David Hoyt moved from San Francisco to Atlanta only a year ago and now has three communes and a cadre of 70 evangelizing disciples there, and centers in three other Southeastern cities. Much of the movement's main strength, however, has been built where it started, along the West Coast.

Some of the manifestations there could command places in William James' *Varieties of Religious Experience*. R.D. Cronquist, for instance, was a carpenter until last July, dabbling on the side in ministerial work. Now the mustachioed, goateed Cronquist is the pastor of the Grace Fellowship

Chapel, a windowless, corrugated shed on a hill in Imperial Beach, Calif. A drab shell, perhaps, but a pearl inside; as one 22-year-old girl put it, 'the heaviest place I know to worship'. Services include free-form 'singing in the spirit', a mighty babble of moans, groans and cries against a background of organ music; 'prophecies', in ersatz King James style; and long Cronquist sermons, complete with angels and demons.

Up the beach at Encinitas is a brand of Christianity that is pure California. Ed Wright, 26, owner of the Sunset Surf Shop and principal apostle of the Christian Surfers, tells how Jesus adds a special dimension to the sport. 'It's so beautiful when you are with the Lord and catch a good ride. When you are piling out for the next one you just say "Thank you Lord for being so good to us and for the good waves and the good vibes".' Christ is the essential focus, though. Surfer Mike Wonder, a fellow convert, sought Christ after he found the perfect wave in Hawaii and it failed to bring him happiness.

Nothing except Christ makes waves at gatherings of Berkeley's Christian World Liberation Front, which was in the vanguard of the movement in the San Francisco Bay Area. CWLF Bible meetings are like an understanding embrace: the members sit naturally in a rough circle; a spaced-out speed freak crawls in, is casually accepted, kneels; a baby plays; the only black plucks a guitar, and the group swings easily into a dozen songs. The hat is passed with a new invitation: 'If you have something to spare, give; if you need, take.' Finally they rise, take one another's hands and sing 'We will walk with each other/We will walk hand in hand/And they'll know we are Christians by our love.'

Spokane's Voice of Elijah spreads the spirit in large ways and small. When house members heard of a hungry old woman who had been cut from welfare, they took up a $42 collection at the I Am coffeehouse, left her groceries, cash and a message that read simply 'from Jesus'. The house reaches large groups through its hard-rock band, the Wilson McKinley, which recently helped draw 8,000 to a 'Sweet Jesus Rock Concert' at Stanford University. The Jesus People almost lost the crowd when one evangelist told the collegians they should 'abstain from sexual immorality, and that means abstain except in marriage. We're finding this is the last area people want to give up.' There were no cheers but, astonishingly in the Age of Aquarius, no hoots either.

Music, the lingua franca of the young, has become the special medium of the Jesus movement. *Godspell*, a bright, moving musical written by students and based on the *Gospel According to St. Matthew*, is a sellout hit off-Broadway. The rock opera *Jesus Christ Superstar*, bound for Broadway next fall, is already a bestselling record album; at New York City's Fifth Avenue Presbyterian Church recently, a minister smilingly baptized a baby 'In the name of the Father, the Holy Ghost, and Jesus Christ Superstar.' *Amazing Grace, Put Your Hand in the Hand* and *My Sweet Lord* are top-40 hits, and Jesus-rock groups, most of them converts, roam the country under such names as Hope, Dove and The Joyful Noise.

Go Tell About Jesus

The sounds produced by the rock groups are not always good nor the lyrics always effective evangelism, but the best of the Jesus-rock music is both professionally and theologically solid. Larry Norman, probably the top solo artist in the field, attacks the occult in his album *Upon This Rock*: 'Forget your hexagram/You'll soon feel fine/Stop looking at the stars/You don't live under the signs.' Many Jesus-rock musicians commit their lives as well as their talent. Drummer Steve Hornyak, 30, of The Crimson Bridge, gave up a $35,000 house, a Toronado, and a career as a school-band director when another Jesus musician challenged him to 'go tell about Jesus'. Scott Ross, 31, a former New York disk jockey, has become head of a Christian commune in Freeville N.Y., the Love Inn. Ross still tapes a weekly show that he uses to promote Jesus music on standard stations.

A growing number of musical stars, including Johnny Cash and Eric Clapton, are among the Jesus movement converts. Paul Stookey of Peter, Paul and Mary has preached on the steps of Berkeley's Sproul Hall; Jeremy Spencer of Britain's Fleetwood Mac has joined the ultrarigid Children of God. Few are more zealous than Pat Boone: he has baptized more than 200 converts in his own swimming pool during the past year.

The revolutionary word is also spread by a growing, literally free Jesus press that now numbers some 50 newspapers across the country. Donations are apparently enough to print 65,000 copies of *Right On!* in Berkeley and 400,000 copies of the *Hollywood Free Paper*, the movement's largest. Now Berkeley's CWLF is hoping to start a Jesus news service. There is much to report, in all parts of the US. Items:

■ At First Baptist Church in Houston, youth-minded Pastor Bisagno, 37, brought in Evangelist Hoag to recruit the young in a week-long revival. Hoag traveled from school to school with his plea, and 11,000 young people stepped forward at Bisagno's church to declare themselves for Jesus. Now the first few pews at First Baptist are reserved for the youngsters. While the rest of the congregation mumble their amens, the kids punctuate Bisagno's sermons with yells of 'Outta sight, man, bee-yoo-ti-ful'.

■ In Chicago's Grant Park bandshell, Street Evangelist Arthur Blessitt last month warmed up a crowd of nearly 1,000 with a lusty Jesus cheer, then led them off on a parade through the Loop, gathering people as they went. 'Chicago police, we love you!' they shouted to cops along the route. 'Jesus loves you!' Blessitt also passed a box through the crowd, asking for a special contribution: drugs. The box came back filled with marijuana, pills and LSD; it was turned over to the flabbergasted cops. This month, Blessitt is really testing Jesus' power. He is in New York City for a three-month blitz among the pimps, prostitutes and porno shops of Times Square for which he hopes to recruit as many as 3,000 young helpers. So far he has had only one unnerving setback. A streetwalker told him that she had worn one of his bright red stickers (TURN ON TO JESUS) and 'never had a better night'.

■ On a cul-de-sac beach at Corona del Mar, Calif., the Rev. Chuck Smith recently held another of the mass baptisms that have made his Calvary Chapel at Santa Ana famous. Under a setting sun, several hundred converts waded into the cold Pacific, patiently waiting their turn for the rite. On the cliffs above, hundreds more watched. Most of the baptized were young, tanned and casual in cut-off blue jeans, pullovers and even an occasional bikini. A freshly dunked teen-ager, water streaming from her tie-dyed shirt, threw her arms around a woman and cried, 'Mother, I love you!' A teen-age drug user who had been suffering from recurring unscheduled trips suddenly screamed, 'My flashbacks are gone!' As the baptisms ended, the crowd slowly climbed a narrow stairway up the cliff, singing a moving Lord's Prayer in the twilight.

■ At Novato, Calif., the new Solid Rock house is perhaps typical of the communal Christian houses. Though none is quite the same as another, they all insist that premarital sex and drugs are out, and many have quite strict rules: up early, to bed by ten or eleven, assigned chores, a certain number of mandatory Bible readings or prayer gatherings. Yet they generally are happy places. 'It is a gentle place, this Solid Rock', reports TIME Correspondent Karsten Prager. 'The voices are quiet, the words that recur are "love" and "blessing" and "the Lord" and "sharing" and "peace" and "brothers and sisters".' Twelve 'brothers and sisters' live in Solid Rock, six men, four women, two babies, the children of unmarried mothers. The men of the commune work at house painting and construction to meet the bills, but the main business of the house is to order the lives within it around Christ. One of the mothers describes the success of that effort simply: 'When I first came to the house, I didn't know Jesus. But it turned out that I grew. I guess I trust now.'

TV and Grass

The path to the movement, in or out of communes, is often littered with drugs. The Way, an 18-year-old, offbeat and minor theological group now virtually taken over and greatly expanded by the Jesus People, has two staunch supporters in Wichita, Kans.: prominent Lawyer Dale Fair and his wife, who got involved when a Way evangelist helped their daughter off drugs. One of the San Francisco pioneers, Ted Wise, has been so successful with drug cures that he now has a new clinic in Menlo Park. Washington, DC, movement leader Denny Flanders tells drug users: 'You can use drugs after Jesus, but you won't need them. If you become Christians this is what has to happen.' Convert Connie Sue McCartney, 21, of Louisiana, describes how 'the devil came to me' and tempted her to return to speed. She had kept some in hand just in case, but she was up to the temptation: 'I took it, flushed it down the john in the name of the Father, the Son and the Holy Ghost.' Former Houston Speed Freak Terry Vincent says: 'Man, God turned me around from the darkness to the light. That's all I know. That is all I want to know.'

Drug cures are not the only attraction for conversion. There are a disproportionate number of Roman Catholics among the Jesus People, attracted by the movement's direct approach to Christ. Many Jews have also joined, claiming that they are not quitting but fulfilling their Judaism. Few spiritual Odysseys, though, are as circuitous as that of Christopher Pike, 21, the younger son of the late Episcopal Bishop James A. Pike. In 1967 he began combining marijuana highs with nonstop television watching: 'TV and grass, that was my god', he says. Then came acid, Eastern religion and Bible reading – while stoned. Recalls Chris: 'One day I saw Ted Wise speaking in Sproul Plaza at Berkeley. He was the first intelligent Christian I ever saw.' Soon thereafter, he made a commitment: 'I just said, "Jesus Christ, I'm going to give myself to you and nobody else". Nothing happened, but I knew. I knew he had reached down, and I was saved.' Now Chris lives in a trailer near Reno, studying religious books and working on a library of religious tapes. 'The old Chris Pike died back there', says the Bishop's son. 'I'm a new creature.'

Many conversions seem to be like Pike's: slow, but finally confident turnarounds rather than lightning-bolt illuminations. Yet some do come suddenly. Marsha Daigle, Catholic and a doctoral student at the University of Michigan, was deeply distraught at the deaths of Martin Luther King Jr. and Robert Kennedy. One day she opened a Bible and suddenly 'knew Christ was my personal Saviour. It was the last thing I expected.'

Gospel Crusaders

Another major part of the Jesus movement is the highly organized, interdenominational youth movement of the established churches – a sort of person-to-person counterpart of mass-rally evangelism. Though they have been around for decades, supported by local congregations and generous private contributors, they are finding a huge new growth in the Jesus revolution.

The biggest of the straight groups is Campus Crusade for Christ, 20-year-old soul child of former Businessman; Bill Bright. He still means business: this year's budget is $12 million, and by next month he will have 3,000 full-time staffers on 450 campuses. Inter-Varsity Christian Fellowship is a different breed of campus evangelism – more intellectual, more socially concerned – but it has no lack of gospel zeal. It conducted a missionary convention at the University of Illinois last December that drew 12,000, probably the largest college religious meeting in North American history. Young Life, founded in 1941, reaches its audience with 1,300 clubs, US and foreign. Youth for Christ began business a few years later with a lanky young evangelist named Billy Graham; it is now in 2,700 high schools.

Extraordinary Love

Few groups have had more impact than has one man, Assemblies of God Minister David Wilkerson, whose growing movement began with a single incident: his dramatic conversion of Brooklyn Teen-Age Gang Lord Nicky Cruz in 1958. Cruz himself is now an evangelist. Wilkerson's evangelical and anti-drug organization, Teen Challenge, has 53 centers. His book about Cruz's conversion, *The Cross and the Switchblade*, has sold 6,000,000 copies; a movie version, starring Pat Boone as Wilkerson will be released nationwide July 1. The book had an unusual side effect: its Pentecostal flavor helped launch the Roman Catholic Pentecostal movement.

Catholic Pentecostalism? The name is an apparent contradiction in terms: an austere and ritualized church coupled with a movement characterized in its early years by unleashed emotionalism – eye-rolling ecstasies, shouting, jumping, even rolling on the floor. Classic Pentecostalism has since toned down markedly, but it can still put even an unwary Catholic into theological shock. Jerry Harvey, who helped start the growing Catholic Pentecostal group in the San Diego area, once invited some Protestant Pentecostalists 'to show us how to do it their way. The poor nuns who were there actually turned white.'

The Catholic establishment in the US has not blanched, but it has not turned red with enthusiasm, even though Pope John XXIII himself called upon the Holy Spirit to 'renew your wonders in this, our day, as by a new Pentecost'. An inquiry conducted in the US for the National Conference of Catholic Bishops did find, however, that Pentecostal experience often 'leads to a better understanding of the role the Christian plays in the Church'. The evidence supports that finding. One Los Angeles priest says that he has stayed in the priesthood because of the 'tremendous peace' he found in the renewal movement. Dr James McFadden, 40, dean of Michigan's pioneering School of Natural Resources, is a Catholic for whom religion 'never had an experiential dimension. It was intellectual, the distant Christ of history.' But he found 'extraordinary' love among the 300 Pentecostals of the university's Word of God community. 'Very few people live as though there really is a God who sent his only son to be a man.'

The Pentecostalist fervor has been growing rapidly. From its beginnings at Duquesne University in 1967, where Wilkerson's book was one of the influences, the movement spread to Notre Dame and Ann Arbor, which have been major forces in it ever since. But there are sizable numbers elsewhere. On Trinity Sunday last week, 450 Catholic Pentecostals held a 'Day of Renewal' at St Theresa Catholic Church in San Diego; this weekend 3,000 Catholic Pentecostals from all over the country are expected to gather at Notre Dame for their annual national conference.

Despite the evidence of enriched religiosity, there is enough in the Catholic Pentecostalist movement to account for the hierarchy's reserve. It is casually ecumenical. Its speaking in tongues – glossolalia, a form of prayer that is usually a babbling non-language – is done quietly, but it is done. The Pentecostals have the unhappy faculty of offending both liberals and conservatives in Catholicism: liberals resent their insistent orthodox theology, conservatives their communal life-style.

Passive v. Ecstatic

The confident conviction of the Jesus revolution (we have the answer; the rest of the world is wrong) irritates many, whatever branch of the movement it radiates from. Dan Herr, publisher of the progressive Catholic bimonthly *The Critic*, calls Catholic Pentecostalism 'spiritual chic'. Some who turn off may be expressing the natural and inevitable resentment of the passive believer against the ecstatic believer. In his magisterial study *Enthusiasm*, the late Catholic scholar Msgr. Ronald Knox described the attitude of the religious enthusiast toward the world at large: 'He will have no weaker brethren who plod and stumble, who (if the truth must be told) would like to have a foot in either world, whose ambition is to qualify, not to excel. He has before his eyes a picture of the early Church, visibly penetrated with supernatural influences; and nothing else will serve him for a model.'

Others criticize the absolutism of the Jesus revolution and the complete dependency it creates in some of its adherents. Jean Houston, director of the Foundation for Mind Research in New York City, finds that while 'the Jesus trip gives them rich expectations and more rigid values, they also suffer a narrowing of conceptual vision. They become obsessed.' She cites the case of one girl who turned to the Jesus movement after a severe family crisis. 'She escaped her guilt and horror, but it had the effect of a psychological and social lobotomy. Where once she had been superbly inquisitive, she now could relate things only in terms of her religion – but she had a focal point for all her energy.' Sociologist Andrew Greeley calls Catholic Pentecostalism the 'most vital movement in Catholicism right now', but warns that it could become 'just pure emotion, even a form of hysteria'. The Rev. George Peters of the United Presbyterian Church says of the Jesus People: 'I see dangers. This biblical literalism. The kids quote verses without understanding them to prove a point. I thought we'd outgrown that. I'd like to see some kind of form.'

The established churches may not have the luxury of choosing the youngsters' style. Whatever the excesses or shortcomings of the Jesus revolution, organized religion cannot afford to lose the young in numbers or enthusiasm. In parts of the movement, of course, the churches are not losing them; indeed, they are gaining zealots. Catholic Pentecostals and straight evangelicals are already having an effect; if organized religion embraced the Jesus People as well, the greening effect on the churches could be considerable. Theologian Martin Marty of the University of Chicago Divinity School feels that the Jesus People, frustrated by a complex society that will not yield to their single-minded devotion, may well disband in disarray. But even Marty says: 'Five years from now you may have some better Presbyterians because of their participation in the Jesus movement.' And the Rev. Robert Terwilliger of New York City's Trinity Institute says longingly: 'There is a revival of religion everywhere – except in the church.'

Sometimes the church is not at fault. When young people began to come into the smoothly running, upper-middle-class congregation at La Jolla (Calif.) Lutheran Church, Pastor Charles Donhowe started evening meetings for them. Soon Donhowe had two congregations, the regular Sunday-at-11 variety and the new Christians in the evening. A minister for nine years, Donhowe was in effect converted by the youngsters to unstructured Christianity. He resigned and took his evening congregation with him. Some of his older parishioners joined the secession. Now known simply as 'Bird Rock', they meet in Bird Rock Elementary School in La Jolla. If Bird Rock is an omen, it would be an ironic one: the dove, after all, is the ancient symbol of the Holy Spirit, and Jesus built his own church upon a *rock*.

The Fact of Faith

There are better omens in the actions of clergymen like Houston's John Bisagno, even when they are uncertain of the full meaning and the life span of the Jesus revolution. Says Bisagno: 'All I know is that kids are turning on to Jesus. My concern is that the staid, traditional churches will reject these kids and miss the most genuine revival of our lifetime.' Canon Edward N. West of Manhattan's Episcopal Cathedral of St John the Divine has also made his church a haven for religious enthusiasts whom he sometimes does not fully comprehend. He says: 'There is no place left where they can go and sort themselves out unless the churches are open. They do an enormous amount of praying, sometimes in the lotus position. One young man comes in and plays the bass recorder. He and God have some relationship over a bass recorder. I don't understand it, but that's his thing.'

In a world filled with real and fancied demons for the young, the form their faith takes may be less important than the fact that they have it. Ronald Knox, who set out in *Enthusiasm* to expose the heresies of religious enthusiasts, concluded by praising their spirit. 'How nearly we thought we could do without St Francis, without St Ignatius', he ended his work. 'Men will not live without vision; that moral we would do well to carry away with us from contemplating, in so many strange forms the record of the visionaries.' Enthusiasm may not be the only virtue but, God knows, apathy is none at all.

Many Things to Many Men

Jesus once asked his disciples, 'Who do men say that I am?' Even they argued uncertainly about the answer – until the Resurrection. In the nearly 2,000 years since, conflicting answers about the nature of Jesus have never stopped coming in. In the past century alone, some 60,000 books have sought to explain Christ. In one of the latest, Journalist William Emerson Jr. complains that in different centuries and cultures people have always concocted 'the sort of Jesus they could live with'. He then goes on to create a gee-whizzy, headline-seeking Christ who traveled the revival circuit.

The traditional view of Jesus is founded on the New Testament and the theological debates that enlivened the first three centuries of the Christian era. A series of church councils early condemned two extreme views: 1) the idea that Jesus was merely a man, and 2) the belief that he was a God who only appeared to be in human form. The orthodox consensus, of course, was that he was both truly man and truly God. Beyond that basic tenet, however, different cultures through the ages have invariably given Christ different characterizations. The medieval church saw him as the ideal knight in the spiritual guidebook *Ancrene Wisse*, and later as Christ the King – a connotation that happened to fit in nicely with the papacy's temporal claims.

Writers in every era have remade Jesus in the image that suited their personal or literary needs. In Milton's *Paradise Regained*, Christ is an intellectual who disdains 'the people' as 'a herd confus'd, a miscellaneous rabble who extol things vulgar'. The 19th century skeptic Swinburne had a character say of Jesus, 'O pale Galilean; the world has grown grey from thy breath.' D.H. Lawrence equated the Resurrection with Jesus' awakening sexual desire. In the 1960s, S.G.F. Brandon saw the Nazarene as a sympathizer of the 1st century's Zealot guerrillas.

*

Artistic interpretations have varied as widely. The painters of the Byzantine era produced a formidable otherwordly Christ; in the Middle Ages he became the stern ruler at the Last Judgment. Gradually, a more human Jesus appeared. Rembrandt scoured the Jewish quarter to find models. By the 20th century, Picasso was painting Jesus as a bullfighter.

While the artistic images of Christ varied, the basic theological view of Jesus as both God and man remained largely unchanged for 1,300 years. Then the empiricism of the 18th century Enlightenment began eroding belief in the supernatural. The New Testament was described as a hodgepodge that revealed much about St. Paul and the early church but little about the real Jesus. In the 19th century, Albrecht Ritschl, a leader of liberal theology, totally rejected the deity of Jesus, and Historian Bruno Bauer denied that the human Jesus had ever lived. In Rudolf Bultmann's 20th century view, the 'Christ of faith' returned, but the 'Jesus of history' was inaccessible. The pendulum is still swinging. Bultmann's disciples have since decided that some of Jesus' actual words and works can indeed be determined through research. Quite a few reputable scholars now believe that the New Testament account is reliable history.

*

America, the land of revivalism, has from the start alternated in its view between an awesome Christ and an accessible Christ. In the Calvinism of the original Great Awakening, Jesus was a severe judge; Jonathan Edwards and others emphasized sinful man's utter helplessness before him. In the 19th century revivals of Charles G. Finney and Dwight L. Moody, however, the Lord had become more sympathetic: he began to help those who helped themselves by responding to his grace. Pious white Sunday-school art has since made Jesus into an effete Aryan rather than a rugged Jewish carpenter, but that image is hardly more subjective than the contemporary Black Jesus in a dashiki. No more biblically authentic is a recent Presbyterian-Methodist TV spot: Jesus fends off the accusers of the Bible's adulterous woman, but the script omits his admonition: 'Sin no more'.

However Christ is viewed, his figure has walked through the ages with a commanding, if sometimes mysterious, presence. For modern man, it is not always easy to understand the Jesus who claimed: 'I am the way and the truth and the life; no one comes to the Father but by me' (John 14:6). Thus it is not at all surprising that the questions that have engaged theologians through the centuries have become pop theology in the rock opera *Jesus Christ Superstar* [...]

C12 Ted Patrick, *Let Our Children Go!*

From T. Patrick and T. Dulack (1976) *Let Our Children Go!*, New York, E.P. Dutton, pp.37, 75–7.

TED PATRICK: I never planned to be a deprogrammer. It's not a job I applied for, and in the beginning I never imagined I'd be in it for four years, deprogramming and arranging for the deprogramming of over one thousand Americans, rescuing them from religious cults. It's not a job I want to continue to do. But until now [the fall of 1975] no one else has been willing to step forward and rectify a dangerous situation in this country which I believe poses threats and challenges to the core of our way of life. Until someone does, I feel I have no choice except to continue in my work.

In the summer of 1971 I was Governor Ronald Reagan's Special Representative for Community Relations in San Diego and Imperial counties in southern California. It was an interesting and demanding job which cast me in the role of a sort of ombudsman, fielding complaints, answering questions, cutting through bureaucratic red tape at every level of the government, trying to provide services in general for a very far-reaching constituency from every class, every race, every walk of life. In my three years in that position, I'd worked hard to make myself visible and available. When the cult troubles began to surface, it was logical enough for distraught and frightened parents to come to my office with requests for assistance.

At the time I was absolutely not aware of the existence of any cults, let alone those that were evil in their nature and purposes. I don't think many people were, anywhere in the country. This, in spite of the fact that by the summer of 1971 the cult movement in America was widespread, well-entrenched, and mushrooming rapidly. [...]

Deprogramming, I think, is widely misunderstood – I mean, what I do, what goes on. To read some of the accounts that have been written by reporters who have never witnessed a deprogramming, you would think it was a cross between the Spanish Inquisition and an orgy sponsored by the Marquis de Sade. It's nothing of the kind. Essentially it's just talk. I talk to the victim, for as long as I have to. I don't deny that that's the catch for many people – 'for as long as I have to'. Yes, in some cases that means restraint. Yes, it also means the victim may not be free to leave when he wants to. When a victim is exceptionally vigorous, it may even mean a measure of physical restraint.

But let me say this. The techniques I employ do not in any way approximate or parallel the psychological kidnapping and mind control that the cults employ. The cults strike at random; they will approach anyone anywhere, without regard to the person's age, background, sex, or occupation. When they go out into the streets to witness – which is their dressed-up term for proselytizing (which is only another dressed-up word, in this instance, for psychological kidnapping) – they attempt to snare people indiscriminately. The Children of God, for example, have attempted to recruit children as young as nine years old. Once they get a victim, they consciously and deliberately set about to destroy every normal pattern of living the victim has known; he is separated from his friends, he is turned against his family, he is led to renounce his education, his career, his responsibilities. He is literally robbed of whatever financial assets he may possess, and his parents are as a matter of course blackmailed into contributing large sums of money to the cult merely in order to be occasionally permitted to see their child. He is physically abused and often expected to work as much as twenty hours a day fund-raising for the group. He is frequently undernourished and psychologically manipulated to the degree that he cannot distinguish between reality and the grotesque fantasies and illusions the cult fosters.

He is programmatically turned against his country, taught that patriotism is sinful, the system Satanic. He is urged to become a revolutionary, to destroy the institutions of society in the name of David Berg or some other phony god. Discord, division, hatred, grief – those are what the cults bestow.

Against that, the deprogramming method is first of all very selective. I don't go into a commune and indiscriminately grab the first person I see, as, in effect, the cults do when they are witnessing on the street. The parents of a young person will contact me – usually after months of deliberation, fear and uncertainty. When we take the person into custody he is, admittedly, held against his will. But it's arguable whether at that stage of his indoctrination he can be said to *have* a will, any will, let alone free will in the sense that we normally use that term. Regardless, the child is rarely held in custody by the parents and me for longer than three days. Usually it takes me less than one day to deprogram a person. I've managed to do it on occasion in an hour.

The important things to remember here are how the cults treated the individual, what their motives were, and how we treat him, what our motives are. The child is with his family throughout the process. He is well-fed. While I admit that limiting his sleep is a basic element in deprogramming, he sleeps at least as much as he did in the cult, almost all of which use fatigue as a strategic weapon. I do not brainwash. I ask questions, basically, and I try to show the victim how he has been deceived. Whereas, in the cult indoctrination, everything possible is done to prevent the person from thinking, in deprogramming I do everything I know how to start him thinking.

All deprogramming is is talk – a lot of talk. It only lasts two or three days. Not thirty or forty days as when a person joins a cult. Not three or four years of constant indoctrination and slave labor. I'm criticized for holding these children against their will. But once you go into the Children of God, or the Unification Church, or the Hare Krishna movement, you are not, practically speaking, free to leave either. Now, that seems to suggest I'm fighting fire with fire – or that, at best, I'm no better in my methods than the cults.

But let's look at motives. I do not make money off the deprogrammed person. His parents pay for my travel and living expenses, and whatever other expenses are incurred during the snatch and deprogramming. He certainly does not become a follower of mine, selling plastic flowers in the streets to support me in a life of great luxury. I do not seek to implant in him any dogma, any preconceived or manufactured view or philosophy of life. Once he is deprogrammed he is absolutely free to do whatever he wants to do. Go to school, go to work, lie on a beach and look at the clouds. Whatever. That's none of my business. All I want and all I do is to return to them their ability to think for themselves, to exercise their free will, which the cults have put into cold storage. I thaw them out, and once they're free of the cult, with very few exceptions they begin again to lead productive lives – and not necessarily conformist lives. Deprogrammed people are as various and individualistic as any group in the society. Motives *are* important. The cults' motives are destructive – this can be demonstrated. My motives, I hope I have demonstrated here, have nothing in common with those of the spiritual gangsters who populate outfits like the Children of God.

C13 National Council of Churches, Statement on deprogramming

From J.G. Melton and R.L. More (1982) *The Cult Experience: Responding to the New Religious Pluralism*, Pilgrim, Appendix B, pp.153–4, footnote omitted.

Adopted by the Governing Board of the National Council of Churches, February 28, 1974.

In this country, kidnapping a young person for ransom is a federal crime of utmost seriousness, but kidnapping such a person in order to change his or her religious beliefs and commitments has not thus far actuated federal authorities to invoke the statute. Grand juries have refused to indict and petit juries to convict persons charged with such acts, apparently because done at the behest of parents or other relatives and ostensibly for the good of the victim.

Sometimes the victim is unarguably a minor, subject to the authority of his or her parents. In other instances, the victim is over 25 or 30, clearly an adult competent to make his or her own commitments in religion as in other matters. The rest are between 18 and 21 years of age, and their claims to adulthood are clouded by the vagaries and variety of federal, state and local laws.

The Governing Board of the NCC believes that religious liberty is one of the most precious rights of humankind, which is grossly violated by forcible abduction and protracted efforts to change a person's religious commitments by duress. Kidnapping for ransom is heinous indeed, but kidnapping to compel religious deconversion is equally criminal. It violates not only the letter and spirit of state and federal statutes, but the world standard of the Universal Declaration of Human Rights, which states: 'Everyone has the right to freedom of thought, conscience and religion; this right includes freedom to change his religion or belief, and freedom, either alone or in community with others and in public or private, to manifest his religion or belief in teaching, practice, worship and observance.'

The Governing Board is mindful of the intense anguish which can motivate parents at the defection of their offspring from the family faith, but in our view this does not justify forcible abduction. We are aware that religious groups are accused of 'capturing' young people by force, drugs, hypnotism, 'brainwashing', etc. If true, such actions should be prosecuted under the law, but thus far the evidence all runs the other way: it is the would-be rescuers who are admittedly using force.

The Governing Board recognizes that parents have the ultimate responsibility for the religious nurture of their children until they become adults in their own right, and parents are morally and legally justified in using reasonable force to carry out their responsibility (even if in matters of religion it may be unwise, ineffective or counterproductive). Nevertheless, at some point, young people are entitled to make their own decisions in religion as in other matters. What that point should be may vary from family to family, since emancipation is surely in most cases virtually complete by 18.

The Governing Board has previously urged the right to vote for 18 year-olds and welcomes the action of those states which are making all rights of citizenship effective at 18 rather than 21. The right to choose and follow one's own religion without forcible interference should likewise be guaranteed at least by that age.

Section D MUSIC IN THE SIXTIES

D1 George Martin, 'With our love – we could save the world'

From G. Martin and W. Pearson (1995 edn) *Summer of Love: The Making of Sgt. Pepper*, London, Pan Books, Chapter 15, pp.123–32, first published 1994.

> Maharishi's Academy of Transcendental Meditation is situated on a big flat ledge, like a giant-sized shelf, 150 feet above the River Ganges. The views from this Ashram (that's the name given by the Indians to any holy place, anywhere where people come to study and meditate) are wonderful. You look out over the river, across to the town of Rishikesh and the plains beyond. There are mountains on the other three sides and jungle all about. Colourful peacocks strut about; you see a monkey or two at every glance, staring down at you from almost every branch of the trees.
>
> *Mal Evans,* The Beatles Monthly Book*, May 1968*

George Harrison was what you might call the Beatles' Third Man – always there, yet somehow elusive. Paul had introduced him to John when they were all teenage schoolboys learning chords on their guitars. Unfortunately for him, George was a few, crucially spotty years younger than John. Perhaps because of this age difference, John was condescending towards George in those early days, and this was still apparent when I first met them all. Later on, this uneasiness seemed to evaporate as the business of being a professional Beatle took over. Some undercurrent between the two men may yet have remained to the very end, though: the only people who came to actual blows with one another on 'Let It Be' were John and George.

The electricity that crackled between Paul and John, and that led to such great music, rather left George out in the cold. He had only himself to collaborate with. If he needed help from the other two, they gave it, but often rather grudgingly. It was not so much that Lennon and McCartney did not believe in Harrison; more that their overwhelming belief in themselves left very little room for anything – or anybody – else.

As for my own role, I am sorry to say that I did not help George much with his song writing, either. His early attempts didn't show enormous promise. Being a very pragmatic person, therefore, I tended to go with the blokes who were delivering the goods. I never cold-shouldered George. I did, though, look at his new material with a slightly jaundiced eye.

When he brought a new song along to me, even before he had played it, I would say to myself, 'I wonder if it is going to be any better than the last one?' It was in this light that I looked at the first number he brought me for the *Sgt. Pepper* album, which was 'It's Only A Northern Song'. I groaned inside when I heard it. We did make a recording of it on 14 February, but I knew it was never going to make it.

I had to tell George that as far as *Pepper* was concerned, I did not think his song would be good enough for what was shaping up as a really strong album. I suggested he come up with something a bit better. George was a bit bruised: it is never pleasant being rejected, even if you are friendly with the person who is doing the rejecting. ('It's Only A Northern Song' did see the light of day in the end, on *Yellow Submarine*.)

When he came up with 'Within You Without You', then, as a replacement, it was a bit of a relief all round. He'd composed it after an intense late-night conversation with his mate Klaus Voormann about the meaning of life. This song was really different; and although George had experimented with Indian music quite a bit before *Sgt. Pepper* – the sitar in 'Norwegian Wood' springs to mind – this was the first time he'd devoted an entire track to his obsession.

'Within You Without You' demanded Indian musicians. It was nothing whatsoever like anything John or Paul could have come up with, and in that lay much of its appeal for me. I still didn't think of it as a great song, though (many now do!). The tune struck me as being a little bit of a dirge; but I found what George wanted to do with the song fascinating. It was cosmically different – weird! The lyrics touched on what you might call the metaphysical: the inner meaning of life, and all that kind of thing. And it was deeply anti-establishment.

'Within You Without You', like Paul's 'She's Leaving Home' and 'Yesterday', was a distinctly solo effort. Looking back, these one-offs were early signs of the group's disintegration. The Beatles had been prisoners of their 'Fab Four' straitjacket for about five years – a very long time in pop music, even then. Look at today's charts and see how many people last as long as five years. Five months, in some cases, if that.

When he first played it to me on his acoustic guitar, George made rather a mournful sound: but I was intrigued. He had a host of Indian musicians who were friends of his, some of whom he called in to play a guide rhythm track with him. George loved working with these musicians, and it was fascinating to see how his ideas grew, and how easily he communicated the complex music to them. Indian rhythms can be extraordinarily difficult, and I have a fond memory of George speaking in a strange tongue, emphasizing the accents with a wag of his head – 'Ta-ta ticky ta, ticky tick ta ta' and so on. The Indian musicians cottoned on instantly. It was most impressive. I, too, knew a few of the musicians from the Asian Music Circle in London, because of my previous work with Peter Sellers.

After producing 'Goodness Gracious Me', Peter's big 1960 cod-Indian hit, I'd had the idea to repeat the formula with the song, 'Wouldn't It Be Lovely?' from *My Fair Lady*. Peter thought this was a great hoot. 'We'll give it an authentic Indian backing ...' I said. I contacted the Asian Music Circle, who provided us with sitar and tabla players. There was only one small snag: the sitar player spoke no English. When I explained that I wanted her to play along with the rhythm track of the song we had already recorded, she would start playing as I was speaking. When I called down from the control room for her to play, she would stop. We got it right eventually, but it took a while. I learned a great deal about the sitar, and about Indian music in the process!

But the dilruba player for 'Within You Without You' I had not met, nor had I come across the bowed instrument he was playing. It is a kind of one-string fiddle, which makes characteristic slurps and swooping sounds: to me, it was a completely closed book. 'This one is going to be meaty', I thought to myself.

There is pop music in India, of course, as there is anywhere else; it tends to be film sound-track music. There is also a rich tradition of folk music in the sub-continent, and north and south Indian classical music, each with its own further subdivisions. George had looked into all this pretty thoroughly, and had homed in on Hindustani north Indian classical music as the thing that appealed to him most. This was one of the most ancient forms of music in the world, he told me, mentioned in India's ancient Vedic literature.

What really appealed to George was the sound – the unique sound the instruments made when used in this very ancient tradition. In some mystical way, he told me, he recognized that sound; it was as if he had heard it before.

George understood that in any song written according to the rules of the Vedic tradition the voice and the dilruba should accompany one another in unison. This was true even of what was basically a Western pop tune. It was the instrumentation, not the melody, that made it sound Indian.

So George and I had a difficult task ahead. My job was to add Western strings to the song – that is, to find classically trained European fiddle players (frequently of Jewish stock) and get them to mimic their Indian counterparts. This intrigued me no end. I couldn't wait to see the titanic clash of cultures in the studio! When it came to it, the European string players mingled pretty well with the Indian players, but musically the Europeans were sliding around all over the place. This was especially true in the second, or middle section of 'Within You Without You', where the tabla changes rhythm from a 4/4 to a much more Indian-feeling 5/4 tempo; here, too, the song gets quite fast and tricky. We had a lot of fun getting that right.

We started working on this strange song (which was, incidentally, one of Geoff Emerick's favourites; he loved George's music) on 15 March. It was a long one, at just over five minutes, and it was split into three main parts. Right from the first note, it brims over with Indian instruments: the dilruba, the tamboura drone, the tabla, and the swordmandel – the zither-like plucked instrument we had already used on 'Strawberry Fields Forever'.

When I was about twelve or thirteen I was riding on my bike and I heard 'Heartbreak Hotel' coming out of somebody's house. The sound meant something to me: it just touched me in a certain way and made me want to know about it or follow it. Likewise with Indian music. It didn't make any sense to me, but somewhere inside of me it made absolute sense. It made more sense than anything I had ever heard before.

(George, South Bank Show*)*

When the Indian instrumentalists arrived hot-foot from exotic Finchley they changed the studio scene – bare walls, bare floor, hostile fridge – pretty dramatically. They scattered carpets on the floor, spread hangings, hunkered down, and generally made themselves at home: suddenly we had colour, life and warmth in our normally cold and featureless surroundings.

George, as usual, set joss-sticks smouldering in the corners. He looked a bit like the Lone Ranger, with his Indian friends. Although the other Beatles were there, they stuck around for the fun of it. None of them played or sang a note. In order to get them to play what he wanted, George would simply sing to the Indian musicians, or occasionally pick a few notes on the sitar.

On that very first evening I met Peter Blake. He had come in to the studios to talk to the boys about their ideas for the album cover, which Paul was trying to organize. Peter had never seen a Beatles recording session, and he was amazed. He thought it was a very gentle, very easy way of working. But it was all the music, really: it was George's hypnotic music that induced that strange air of peace.

And so we began recording:

TRACK 1: looking at our recording sheets for 15 March, we started off with a tamboura drone, as you generally have to with any Indian track. Neil Aspinall was ideal for the tamboura drone; he'd got pretty used to stroking this atmospheric instrument – he'd had plenty of practice on *Revolver.* We had several other tambouras going, though, at the same time, to give us depth in the drone.

TRACK 2: tabla, the percussive Indian drum-sound, along with a small amount of swordmandel.

TRACKS 3 and 4: dilruba, carrying the tune.

The song was basically this tune and the accompanying drone – there were no harmonies in it. In Indian classical music the voice is regarded as the primary instrument. All music, according to Vedic thinking, started through the voice – so it followed that all other instruments were made to copy the voice, and not compete with it in any way.

We finished that night at 1.30 a.m., and left the song for exactly one week, until 22 March, while we were occupied with the album cover. Then we dubbed what we had done on to Tracks 1 and 2 of a second four-track tape. The tablas and tambouras we mixed on to one track, the dilrubas on to the other. We added George's vocals, and, when he was not singing, his sitar, on to Track 4. This left Track 3 for my string score, which I still had to write. This 22 March session was another long one, winding up at 2.15 on the morning of 23 March.

We were getting near the end of the album now, but there was still a little way left to go. We came back in on Monday 3 April, at 7 p.m. as usual, to finish off. 'We', in this case, meant George, myself, and the outside musicians – there were no other Beatles present that night.

It turned out to be a marathon eleven-and-a-half-hour session. We worked our socks off in the big studio, No.1, until three in the morning, recording the string score I had written to fit the Indian tracks we had already laid down.

I had eight violinists and three cellists, led again by Erich Gruenberg. They were all first-class players in their own right, and they had to be – they found it very difficult indeed to follow and keep up with the elastic swoops and wiry furrows of the dilruba. It was also pretty tedious for them, having to go over and over the same phrase until George was satisfied with it. By now we had only one track left on the tape, so if we did not get everything right on a given take, we just wiped the entire take.

In short, we had to get it right; but we did a lot of takes before George was pleased with the result. George's meticulousness was worth it, in the end. Gruenberg's gentlemen-players did the business: we had added another dimension to the song.

When George was finally satisfied with what we had achieved it was about 3 a.m., and we all assumed we could go home. The musicians did go, they couldn't wait to go – it was well past their bedtime. To my astonishment, though, George himself wanted to carry on.

Propping our eyelids up with joss-sticks, we moved over to Studio No. 2, across the road, where we spent a further three-and-a-half hours mixing. I eventually got home at seven or so, in time for breakfast. [...]

Despite all our efforts, it still wasn't quite there. So we were back in again that night, at seven, for further mono and stereo mixing until 12.45 the next morning. We did a lot of technical things, like artificially double-tracking the strings, to give them more body. George wanted to dub some laughter on to the end of the song. He didn't want people to feel he was being over-earnest, boring for Britain about the meaning of life, and we found a bit of tape that had the four Beatles cracking up with laughter at the end of some take or other. This spontaneous hilarity was dropped in at the end of the song, and George was happy.

'Within You Without You' is obviously a long way from your normal Western pop song. It has no harmonic structure, no chords, and it doesn't modulate as Western songs generally do. There is the tamboura drone, which gives you a sense of tonality, and the tabla, which gives you a sense of rhythm; but all there is on top of that is the dilruba and vocal line – the tune itself. All the instruments are playing in unison, including the cellos, which are playing an octave lower than the dilruba. Without the strings, the song would have sounded *too* Indian, if anything.

We did make one concession to Western pop music, which was a tiny bit of counterpoint in the melodic line; if you listen, you will hear another line answering it from time to time, but that was the only one.

> ... we've had four years doing what everybody else wanted us to do. Now we're doing what we want to do ... Everything we've done so far has been rubbish as I see it today. Other people may like what we've done, but we're not kidding ourselves. It doesn't mean a thing to what we want to do now.
>
> *George Harrison,* Daily Mirror*, 11 November 1966*

The other Beatles liked 'Within You Without You', though they were a bit bemused by it. But then that was George – always coming up with the unexpected. They thought it was well worth putting in because of its eccentricity alone.

George did plough a lonely furrow in his music. 'Within You Without You' is very introspective: a distillation of George's studies of Eastern philosophy and music. Although Eastern culture became big during the late sixties, George was one of the first to look east, and the depth of his interest in Vedic philosophy put him way beyond the reach of the trendy pack barking behind him.

Despite what I've said about the relatively marginal position that George's music had within the group, it would be entirely wrong to think that he himself was excluded from it. George had something stronger than power: he had influence. Witness the fact that all of the boys followed him to India to sit at the feet of the Maharishi. George tried to persuade me to ease my karma, too, but I excused myself on the grounds of extreme old age.

The Beatles were all looking for something. They had achieved great fame and fortune, but that had made them wonder all the harder what it meant. They were looking for a greater faith than the half-baked versions of Eastern religion and culture circulating in the West could give them. They all wanted to experiment, to push at the envelope of their upbringing, beliefs and culture. They wanted to find out what it was all about.

George was able to answer some of the questions they asked, and the Maharishi seemed to answer more. He was able to bring them a measure of inner peace, which was something they had not found before.

Although they became disillusioned with it afterwards, transcendental meditation was more than a passing fad for the Beatles. It lasted long enough that even after *Sgt. Pepper,* when the Maharishi was visiting Wales, they all rushed off again to sit at his feet. The scales fell from their eyes when it became clear that the guru was after all very much a human being, with feet of clay, but George still to this day will insist: 'OK, that's fair enough, but it doesn't alter the basic truth', by which he means the truths he learned from Eastern philosophies all those years ago.

> The Vedic system is all about enlightenment, basically, and music is one of the vehicles to gain enlightenment.
>
> *George Harrison,* South Bank Show

[...] *Pepper* is a peculiarly English album, despite the exotic flowering of 'Within You Without You'. I suppose it's a bit chicken-and-egg; it is like saying that Mary Quant dresses are 'English'. Well of course they are – she's English. But there is something characteristic of what was happening in England at that time, something in the air that *Pepper,* like a Quant design, expressed. You couldn't have heard anything like *Pepper* from America.

Why? Maybe it is because in spite of their rebelliousness, in spite of their waywardness, in spite of their genius, it was a very disciplined Beatles sound. It was an organized, relatively controlled sound. This is a difficult concept to pin down, but it is like looking at an American car of the time, and then looking at its English counterpart. The American product could be, was often, overblown, over-sized, gross, even, like a Cadillac – all teeth and fins. English cars, on the other hand, tended to be discreetly lined, elegant: the Rolls-Royce Silver Shadow of the time still looks good today.

Pepper has style because it was restrained. It knew when to stop.

D2 Ray Davies, *X-Ray*

From R. Davies (1994) *X-Ray*, Harmondsworth, Penguin, pp.337–9, 346.

As a teenager I had stood on Waterloo Bridge and watched the high tide nearly flood the banks of the Thames. The water was a bright brown; almost red. This was probably caused by pollution, but it gave the impression that the water was like blood flowing through a giant vein that led to the pumping heart of the Empire. I felt that there was a bigger tide coming that would completely flood the banks and submerge the Houses of Parliament. This was a tide of reality and change that was soon to turn England on its head. I started writing a song about Liverpool that implied that the era of Merseybeat was coming to an end, but I changed it to 'Waterloo Sunset' not only because that gave me a bigger canvas to work on but because it was about London, the place where I had actually grown up. We tried recording the song with Shel, but I felt so precious about it that I pretended that it was an experiment for an album track which had not worked. We played the back track a couple of times but gave up before anybody had a chance to hear the melody or lyrics properly. [...]

[...] in early April I went back into the studio and laid down the back track. I remained so secretive about 'Waterloo Sunset' that I would not even sing the lyrics while the band played. I went home and polished up the lyrics until they became like a pebble which had been rounded off by the sea until it was perfectly smooth. A week later I went into the studio with Dave for a couple of hours to put on his guitar part, which I had carefully prearranged in my plodding piano style at home. On 13 April I took Rasa, Pete and Dave into number 2 Studio at Pye and we stood round the microphone and put on our backing vocals. I still didn't tell them what the lyrics would be about. Simply because I was embarrassed by how personal they were and I thought that the others would burst out laughing when they heard me sing. It was like an extract from a diary nobody was allowed to read. But when I finally put the vocal on later that evening everything seemed to fit and nobody laughed. [...] Terry meets my imaginary Julie on Waterloo Bridge, and as they walk across the river darkness falls and an innocent world disappears. [...]

The lyric told how the imaginary Julie, who suddenly symbolized England, met my nephew, Terry, on Waterloo Bridge. A reunion of past and future that had obviously never happened. I thought about Terry's father Arthur, and how his bitterness and sense of betrayal by Britain had forced him to emigrate to Australia to a new life. For the first time, I considered the possibility that Arthur may have been right.

D3 Ray Davies, 'Waterloo Sunset'

From R. Davies (1997) *Waterloo Sunset*, Viking, pp.233–40.

The day was blurred. Like one of those old French Impressionist paintings where you're never sure whether the artist was drunk or needed spectacles. Fox strolled across his attic room to read the letter by the one dormer window. He peeled open the buff envelope and saw the hospital's headed paper. He set a kettle to boil. Normally he would hover impatiently, but today, he had more time. He listened intently as the water started to boil, then studied the steam as it curled out of the spout, until the force of the boiling water made the kettle splutter and shake. He'd never stopped to consider the physical process before. Full-fat milk. No need to worry about cholesterol now. He hadn't bothered to read the diagnosis when it had first arrived. He'd left it on the table at the side of his bed, and it had sat there like an unwanted intruder. He didn't know why he should read it today. He knew the contents: Results positive. Only the punctuation registered. The commas, a chance to take a breath or pause; the full stops, the end of a phase. Fox's body was coming to a full stop. He was in his final phase. Danger and the risk of death had been part of his life. The GBH and then the robberies. What he found difficult now was the clinical assessment, the parcelling out of time. It was as if there was an assassin waiting in the dark. He drank the tea as if it was his last. Looked at the world through his window and, back inside, through the frames of his paintings. He had imagined those worlds. They were places he had never been, the chronicle of his imagination in prison.

Fox considered himself a Londoner. Apart from a spot of porridge in Dartmoor and that awful time in Rampton, he'd lived in London all his life. But there were so many places he had never been – the Tower of London, the Houses of Parliament, Westminster Abbey. Overfamiliarity led him to take them for granted, even after years in prison. The marks persisted. His once elegant hands, an artist's hands maybe, fingers bloated by too many fights. He'd never let himself go to seed, even now he was on the way out. Cleanliness had helped him keep his dignity. It hadn't moved him any closer to godliness, though. He'd resisted the chaplain's persuasion, but now he wished he hadn't given religion such a wide berth. What would be left of him when he was gone?

He remembered the old song about two characters, Terry and Julie, who met at Waterloo Underground. The song had come on the radio while he was waiting in the get-away car at the Cannon Street robbery. He had been engrossed in it and hadn't noticed the police cars draw up. One of the policemen whistled the song as he took him into custody. A painting of that song should have begun his chronicle, but it had always eluded him. Maybe he should try once more.

He headed for the Embankment. It was undergoing a face-lift. The Houses of Parliament had been cleaned up, and the new site for Charing Cross station was nearly complete. The skyline was being altered by high-rise office blocks, but the Savoy still retained its dingy elegance. Fox wanted to convey a feeling of romance, but somehow he found himself concentrating on the isolated people walking along by the river instead of the warm feeling the song's imagery gave him. The people seemed lost, the same way Fox felt. He thought of the bag-woman he'd painted in Regent's Park. When he got back to his flat and tried to work on the picture, he got depressed. There seemed to be nothing but these sad people, the scene itself had no life of its own, no poetry. Maybe it was best left as an idea, maybe it couldn't be captured in an image. Suddenly, Fox felt pain shoot through his body. In his obsession with the painting he'd forgotten his illness. He had medication, but his body must have been becoming immune to it. He doubled the dosage and washed it down with half a bottle of vodka. The cocktail dulled the pain, but the bitterness seized him inside. Sod art. He was only a third-rate amateur. He wouldn't be remembered for his painting. He was a con artist. One last job. He'd have to spruce himself up.

He wandered down Marylebone High Street and saw a tuxedo in the window of a charity shop. It would be perfect. Next to it, on a mannequin, was an old ballroom gown, just like his mother used to wear. Sequins sewn on by hand, sections of lace, old embroidery. Slightly see-through – that must have raised the blood pressure of many a dance partner. He remembered that night. Fox and his mates had been jiving to rock and roll records, but had stopped dead in their tracks when his mum and dad had started waltzing. They seemed so affectionate, so in love. The tuxedo fitted Fox perfectly. The trousers were a little shiny on the backside, but otherwise the tux was in mint condition. There was a man's name inside, next to the maker's label. Geoffrey Sillet. Only a name. It said nothing about the person's life. Still, it was a good deal, and it made him feel debonair. Now, he'd be able to con his way back in with the high rollers.

It may have been the effects of the medication, but Fox could have sworn the doorman of the Savoy bowed as he walked in. It was like he was floating. The lobby was packed, but somehow the crowd parted as Fox waded through. Surely there would be some unsuspecting toff in the bar who Fox could take advantage of. Some eager do-gooder primed for a soft touch. He sat down next to a cultivated-looking type who was dressed for dinner. He was chain-smoking. Fox sized him up. He ordered a lager, and the man started talking to him. His name was Richard. There was a world of difference in their accents, but as Richard spoke Fox's initial dislike disappeared. He felt some empathy for the man. He was in the middle of a rather difficult negotiation and was waiting to meet a business partner in the bar. He seemed to identify with Fox too. They shared their cynicism for a world that seemed full of double standards. Fox talked about his life, how he had been repatriated through art. Richard talked about class. Even though he had been to a smart public school, he never finished 'the course'. He felt under-educated, out of step with people from the same background. He hadn't gone to university, hadn't gone for a safe establishment job. He envied people who made a living out of being creative. They filled all the gaps in his life, and helped uproot a society that appalled Richard. He'd been ostracized, but was happy to be an outsider. Money was a way of getting back. Fox couldn't have agreed more. This guy would be easy. Richard continued.

'I met this chap a while ago. Tracked him down in New York. He was a total wreck. Haunted, a little deranged. We came from totally different backgrounds and had nothing to connect us, but we both wore the same shirts, and that was enough. Somehow that gave us an insight into one another. We were meant to go on a journey together.'

Fox watched Richard as he searched his jacket pockets for a cigarette. He caught a glimpse of his wallet.

'The only problem was, neither of us was sure who was taking who. We envied each other's lives. He wanted my ability to do a deal, I wanted his creativity. Our meeting was premature, but we learned a great deal from each other. He confided many of his secrets to me. It turned out he was not quite the person I thought he was. Something in him had gone astray. Some sort of personal trauma that was too painful to confront.

He'd gone inside his work so deeply, he'd surrendered his own character to his songs, and they lived through him instead of the other way around. He had become the characters he had invented. The lyrics in his songs spoke for him. He lost his own voice.

'I inherited only the shell. I tried to connect it with his everyday persona, and sometimes it seemed to work, but I always knew that the real creative part of him was down in the Underground, busking anonymously, away from the spotlight. That way he could sing songs about people without getting involved in their lives and getting hurt. Now, we have simply brought each other to this place, but still neither of us knows who is taking who.'

The bar was getting crowded. Richard's mysterious business partner still hadn't arrived, and he suggested that he and Fox take some air. They walked up the Strand, past Charing Cross, and looked at the river. The rush-hour traffic was in full flow, and the commuters were making their way across the bridge. Fox found himself being seduced by the view of London he'd been trying to capture. Richard was still smoking. He was talking about the river, saying he believed that it would always lead him to good fortune. They walked on, and reached a dark stairwell under Charing Cross Bridge. Fox felt it was time to take advantage.

'Could do with some good fortune myself.'

A stab of pain stopped him from overpowering his victim, and now Fox was helpless. Richard helped him up the steps, to the top of the bridge. Fox could hardly get the words out.

'I'm going to die.'

Richard smiled compassionately. His words shot through Fox more powerfully than the pain.

'You've actually been dead a while. You've just been waiting to be taken captive. In a moment. Like one of the pictures you paint.'

'Then why am I here? What am I waiting for?'

'You are waiting for that final moment. But you won't know for sure until you see that river stop. That's when you'll know he's finished. Your song is done and you can go home. Try not to build your hopes up. You're probably just another unresolved idea that will get shelved for another time. You'll be hanging around on this bridge for ever I expect. Just like me.'

Fox was grappling with what Richard was saying.

'You mean there's no escape?' Richard sighed.

'I thought there was once. I thought I'd made my fortune and would be sailing around the world on my yacht.'

Fox's face lit up.

'You have a yacht?'

'Yes. She's been having some repairs done. She's already left Miami without me. I thought she'd be my get-away. Unfortunately, it looks as though the next time I'll see her is when we sail up the River Thames.'

Fox came to a conclusion which alarmed him.

'Did you mention this yacht to this friend of yours?'

'Only in passing. Why?'

'No reason really. It just makes sense now how I decided one day to paint a picture. I'd never seen racing yachts but the image just came into my head. Sold the picture to a young couple for a tenner.'

Richard raised an eyebrow.

'Yes. Probably part of his plan.'

'Is that why I am here? So you can show me the way?'

Richard looked at Fox's tuxedo.

'Hardly think so. Although you do seem dressed for the occasion. Someone will recognize you by the tuxedo. They'll be dressed in one too. Probably by the same tailor.'

Fox felt dizzy and confused. Maybe it was the medication. Richard carried on talking.

'The lost people travel around on the same journey for ever. Trapped in their own hell on the Underground. It's not until they come up to the overground that they see the chance to be free. You see the people standing on the bridge looking at the river? They see their whole life flowing down that river and they come, and they look at it, and they see everything they ever wanted. You'll look at the river. Just stand and watch it flow. Slower and slower until it stops moving. You'll know when the time has arrived. When the river stops. Just blink your eyes once and the image will stay with you.'

The setting sun lit Richard's face with an eerie glow. Fox felt the strength drain from his body.

'I'm not ready. God has no angel to guide me. I'll try and get to the hospital.'

Richard stared at Fox long and hard, and every emotion passed across his face. Then he looked away dispassionately.

'I have to make my appointment.'

Fox was still alert enough to be inquisitive.

'Who are you waiting for?'

'The man who wrote "Waterloo Sunset". I've been trying to coax him across the river. I've been in the bar at the Savoy every night, just as he said, but he never comes. He's not ready to leave the Underground.'

'Maybe I'll see him there', said Fox. 'If I can't paint the picture, I'd like to meet the man who wrote the song.'

'I can't go down to the Underground with you. I spent too much time there.'

'You'll capture the picture in your own imagination, and there will be a space in it for you.'

Fox shook Richard's hand and left him on the bridge, cigarette in hand, looking at the river. Richard seemed at peace. Resigned.

Fox slowly walked across to Waterloo station. He just about managed to climb the steps under the clock and took the escalator down to the Underground. He heard the sound of gentle guitar-playing and was convinced he heard a choir singing. The medication was kidding him. There'd be no angels in hell. As he descended, the choir faded away and the dull roar of the Underground swelled. Fox thought he heard the screams of a torture chamber. Condemned commuters suffering hell's wrath. Or was it a train screeching to a halt? He saw a busker at the end of the corridor. He was singing something about commuters journeying through the underworld.

It sounded as if the lyrics were being sung in another language, but he could still catch the meaning. The busker tilted his head to look over his sunglasses and smiled at Fox. He said something without speaking, and Fox replied without a word. They walked out to Waterloo Bridge. Fox looked into the busker's sunglasses and saw the reflection of the sun setting over Waterloo. Even in the tinted glasses the light was too bright. The whole sky seemed to be on fire. Fox looked towards the brilliant light. He was caught in the moment and the river stopped.

D4   Maggie Parham, 'Max input'

From M. Parham (1994) 'Max input', *The Independent Magazine*, 3 September, pp.36–8.

'Otters Crossing', warns a sign in the Orcadian capital, Kirkwall. It is a quiet place where, for most of the year, otters cross undisturbed; but for a week in midsummer – a time when Orkney spills over with light for almost 24 hours a day – the streets fanning out from Kirkwall's Viking cathedral bristle with artistic life. In June, the BBC Philharmonic Orchestra, slung about with instruments ranging from French horns to flexatones, flew into the city's tiny airport along with a school brass-band from Norway, Asa Briggs and Seamus Heaney. Other summers have brought Vovka Ashkenazy, Julian Bream and the Kings Singers, Isaac

Stern, Mstislav Rostropovich and Ted Hughes. And always, darting among these musical and literary giants like some bright, mercurial creature from *The Wind in the Willows*, is the composer Sir Peter Maxwell Davies.

It is 18 years since Sir Peter – known to all as Max – conceived the idea of bringing world-class musicians and writers to the inhabitants of the Orkney islands through the St Magnus Festival, and 24 years since he first visited the islands and decided to make them his home.

He had come north on holiday with his manager, James Murdoch, and picked up a second-hand copy of George Mackay Brown's *Orkney Tapestry* in the Orcadian seaport of Stromness. 'It was', he says, 'one of the most wonderfully poetic evocations of a place I had ever read.' The next day, 'in a hyper state of tiredness and receptivity to experience', Max took a ferry to the mountainous island of Hoy, and met, by chance, Brown having lunch with a friend, Archie Bevan, in the dark, windswept valley of Rackwick. 'It was', he says, 'one of those days when everything happens as if pre-ordained.'

Max was then 36 years old, a vastly prolific *enfant terrible* who had burst upon the British music scene in the early-Fifties – when Vaughan Williams was regarded as a 'modern' composer – with work that was explosive, atonal and deeply uncosy. To his supporters, he was thrillingly avant-garde; to the Establishment he was, in the words of James Murdoch, 'gay, mad, a witch'. The small group of Orcadians gathered in Rackwick were intrigued: 'It was a dricht, damp day', Archie Bevan remembers, 'and the sea was pounding in. There was virtually no colour in the sky. Max sat there silent, reacting to the sounds.' Brown remembers a 'slight, dark, active man with black curls and intense, smouldering eyes. We liked him, but we thought "for sure, he won't be staying in Rackwick".'

But Max had not only decided, 'instantly', that Rackwick was a place in which he must compose, and that he should set George Mackay Brown's writing to music; he had also spotted, on a cliff overlooking the Atlantic, a deserted croft – doorless, roofless, feet-deep in sheep dung and not for sale – where he determined to live. 'Had I stayed in town at that stage, and not cleared my creative faculties out with big doses of fresh air and sea, I could have got stuck. I could', he repeats, 'have got stuck.'

Max 'stuck' is hard to imagine. On midsummer's day in Archie Bevan's sitting-room in Stromness, he perches on the edge of a sofa like a well-wound spring. The black curls are now heavily frosted with grey – he will be 60 on Thursday, but he fixes me with the same intense, smouldering eyes as he leans forward, waiting for questions. (He claims that once, during a heated discussion with Karlheinz Stockhausen, a wine glass sitting between them inexplicably shattered.)

At the age of four, he explains, he had his first experience of orchestral music at an amateur production of Gilbert & Sullivan's *Gondoliers*, and decided to become a composer. At eight, he wrote his first piece – 'three flats in the key signature, two changes of time'. Since then, he has steamed forward, turning obstacles to his own account, harnessing his formidable energy with ferocious self-discipline and single-mindedness. 'Never marry!' one of his former students remembers him insisting, 'It will distract you from your work.' Max talks in controlled, perfectly articulated sentences, occasionally allowing himself a semi-quaver breath of laughter, becoming more precise when the conversation takes undesired turns.

During a discussion on musical education, for example, and the mess he believes successive governments have made of it, I unwittingly mention Kenneth Clarke. 'Kenneth *who*, did you say?' he asks, coolly polite.

'Kenneth Cla ...'

'Let's not discuss these nonentities. They are despicable, quite beyond any sense, any kind of realisation of human potential. I think I would rather not talk about them.'

But such is Max's hatred of politicians of every complexion that he cannot help but talk about them, again and again. 'We have a government', he says, 'whose low strategies are systematically eroding all the institutions that have made this country great; for whom cultural life is something to be measured in terms of market forces, as if money were the only god at whose altar we should pray. Of course', he continues, 'people have survived far worse things than the disgusting trivialities of Tory politicians, but one can't help feeling a certain despair at the way things are going.' London, he believes, has fallen into 'a state of despondency impossible to express or analyse', but in Scotland, where the population is drawn together by its 'absolute huge hatred' of what is going on in Westminster, he senses some vitality and hope. 'I would like to be a citizen of an independent Scotland within Europe', he says, 'I hope I live to see that.'

The Government is not alone in arousing Max's outrage. We touch on his religious beliefs. Spirituality interests him, but dogma and religious authority are 'utterly wicked', organised religion 'possibly the most evil force in civilisation', and the Pope more dangerous and loathsome even than Kenneth Clarke.

This visceral loathing of authority of any kind has its roots in his schooldays in Manchester. His father, a foreman at a local manufacturing firm, had hoped for a son who would go with him to football matches, but astonished though he was to have produced a child obsessed with music, both he and Max's mother supported his ambition. But the headmaster at his grammar school tried, literally, to beat it out of him: 'He was a very fat man, and I remember him dragging me up to his study and giving me six of the best for playing the piano. "My dear boy", he would say, "this is not a girls' school".' Opposition strengthened his resolve: 'I kept a score hidden on my knee during lessons, and studied in secret for music A-level, then took myself off for the exams at Manchester High School for Girls. When I got a Lancashire County music scholarship, the headmaster claimed credit. It was a great insight into human nature.'

Despite these early struggles, Peter Maxwell Davies has maintained the idealism of someone who has been spared many of life's more mundane aggravations. An adored only child, who realised from the age of 14 that he was homosexual, he has never known the rough-and-tumble compromise of normal family life. For many years, moreover, the burden of his day-to-day administration has been shouldered for him by his manager, Judy Arnold. 'Poor Judy has to cope with all sorts of things while I just bury my head in the sand like an ostrich', he admits, emitting a quick laugh. 'Airlines, hotels, difficult musicians. I don't deal with any of that. Judy has to do it.'

If aloofness from the daily grind has made him an idealist, it has also left him with a refreshingly unjaded, almost childlike, sense of justice, and a determination to work as a thorn in the flesh of the Establishment in defence of his beliefs. Last year, the Arts Council announced that, because of cuts in its funding, two of the big London orchestras would cease to receive grants. In what amounted to an open letter to the Government, Max published a furious, passionately-worded feature in the *Daily Mail*. 'Music and art are what raise us above the apes', he declared. If the grants were cut, then he would leave Britain and renounce his knighthood. 'I don't actually know', he admits, 'if one can renounce a knighthood', but as his threat was followed by an immediate recantation from the Arts Council, it is a ploy he is keeping up his sleeve for future use.

For nearly 15 years, meanwhile, he has battled against a Government threat to introduce open-pit uranium mining on a wild and beautiful stretch of the Orkney coast. 'Long before Chernobyl', he says, 'I'd become concerned about the lies that government after government had put out about nuclear power – that it's going to be cheaper when they've subsidised it up to the hilt, and when their real reason for promoting it is that the side product of producing nuclear power is uranium, which can be used for nuclear warheads.' In 1979, after an announcement that uranium was a national asset over which the people of Orkney had no control, Max set to work on *Black Pentecost*, a bitter, polemical symphony based on George Mackay Brown's novel *Greenvoe*, in which the islands are drilled and gutted in the name of progress. He followed it with the *Yellow Cake Revue*, an anti-nuclear cabaret which he performed for local Orcadians in a pub in Stromness.

'I make myself do these things', Max says, 'because I believe that a composer has a direct responsibility to his community.' It is a responsibility that manifests itself in numerous ways, from getting up on spring nights to help the farmer in Rackwick with lambing, to visiting and composing for the Orcadian school children, to 'sweating blood' to bring art to the islands through the St Magnus Festival. But these things do not come easily – 'by nature', he says, 'I am a very quiet, retiring sort of person who does not like having to deal with a lot of people', and essentially Orkney remains for him a place of solitary hard work and self-examination.

In 1969, the year before he discovered Hoy, Max had reached 'pretty well the limits of my capabilities of expression and expressionism', in a torrent of new works. His ballet, *Vesallii icones*, at the end of which a near-naked dancer emerges from a tomb as the Antichrist and curses Christianity, had been received with a mixture of rapturous applause and shocked dismay. At its Prom première, *Worldes Blis*, his titanic orchestral work, caused many of the audience to walk out booing. At the same time, his house in Dorset and most of his possessions were destroyed in a fire. 'It was one of those strange synchronistic things', he says, 'I realised I had come to the end of a particular line.'

His first year in Orkney, Max 'sat about, listening to the sound of the sea and the sound of the birds and the wind, getting to know myself very well'. His croft was never silent – 'even inside', he says, 'there's always the sound of the sea creating a kind of alien harp effect against the cliffs', – but he found that the suck and crash of the Hoy coast sharpened his concentration. 'It is the aural equivalent', he says, 'of the light which reflects off the sea and puts a halo on visual experience. Everything becomes more intense because of that extraordinary almost subliminal thrumming.'

Gradually, new works began to pour out. Many were inspired by the novels and poetry of George Mackay Brown – 'I almost can't read his work', Max says, 'without imagining music'; many, like his *Kirkwall Shopping Songs, Stone Litany* and *An Orkney Wedding, With Sunrise*, drew directly on his Orcadian experiences. Even in those that did not, the influences of Hoy are discernible. In the dark, second movement of his cello concerto, for example, he depicts with a sudden flashing of violins a sight he caught one morning as a shoal of mackerel swam into Rackwick bay beneath his croft.

Not all Orcadians have taken to this music. One farmer admits he would rather listen to the sea as it is, while a Stromness lady remarked memorably that his work sounds to her like 'a canteen of cutlery falling downstairs'. But to those who have followed his work, Orkney has brought a perceptible change. 'He is no less colourful a composer since he came here', says Dick Hughes, head of music at Kirkwall grammar school, for whom Max has composed an organ sonata, 'but less angry, more accessible, more lyrical'. No longer the high priest of the avant-garde, he has become the grand old man of British music.

This metamorphosis has brought no slackening in pace. In the past eight years, nine Strathclyde Concertos, written for the Scottish Chamber

Orchestra, have appeared with what one critic describes as 'chilling regularity'. Max's diary is full from now until the year 2000. For the week of the Festival, he rushes about Kirkwall with apparently twice the energy of performers half his age, chewing his glasses, seizing every opportunity to enthuse musicians, local Orcadians and members of the public.

Late one morning, between a rehearsal and a performance, Judy Arnold speeds him up to Kirkwall grammar school. Tipping himself back and forth on a plastic school chair, he spends half an hour in the music department, surrounded by teenagers. 'What should I do', asks one pale, red-headed girl, 'if I want to be a composer?' 'Want?', he replies fixing her with an intense stare, 'Wanting is not enough. A composer must be *compelled.*'

Section E ROTHKO AND WARHOL

E1 James Breslin, 'Parnassus on 53rd Street'

From J.E.B. Breslin (1993) *Mark Rothko – A Biography*, Chicago, London, University of Chicago Press, pp.3–7, footnotes omitted.

For eight months during the winter of 1958 and the spring of 1959, Mark Rothko worked, eight hours daily, on a set of murals he had been commissioned to produce for the Four Seasons restaurant in the new Seagram Building being constructed on Park Avenue, between 52nd and 53rd Streets, in New York City. Designed by Philip Johnson, the Four Seasons was to be an exclusive and expensive restaurant where, in Rothko's words, 'the richest bastards in New York will come to feed and show off'.

'I accepted this assignment as a challenge, with strictly malicious intentions,' Rothko declared. 'I hope to paint something that will ruin the appetite of every son of a bitch who ever eats in that room.' More than that, he hoped to make his 'viewers feel that they are trapped in a room where all the doors and windows are bricked up, so that all they can do is butt their heads forever against the wall'. Rothko, who had been butting his own head against the walls of New York's art world for more than thirty years, wanted to make the well-heeled Four Seasons patrons feel just as he did.

His malice was being enacted in a large, 'cavernous' studio, in a former YMCA building. To approximate the interior of the restaurant, Rothko had covered three of the studio's walls, for about two-thirds of the room's twenty-three-foot height, with plasterboard, then built a fourth, movable wooden wall. He had also installed pulleys on the ceiling to allow him flexibility in adjusting the height at which the paintings could be hung. This studio was kept *very* dark. Of its eight windows – all about fifteen feet from the floor – four were blocked off by a storage area Rothko had constructed for his paintings, the lower halves of two more windows were cut off by the plasterboard walls. Only the two northern windows admitted a very dim light. Robert Motherwell described the room as 'a darkened movie set'. Rothko's friend Dore Ashton found 'the great space' as 'dim as a cathedral'. Rothko himself, when he wasn't stressing the malice behind his project, was proclaiming its exalted, even sacred character, as if he were executing paintings for a cathedral rather than a restaurant. When, in the summer of 1959, he visited Pompeii, he claimed 'a deep affinity' between his own murals and those in the House of Mysteries there – 'the same feeling, the same broad expanses of somber color'. At the end of a long afternoon in which he showed the murals to Ashton, Rothko declared: 'They are not pictures. I have made a place.'

At the time of the Four Seasons project, Rothko lived, with his wife, Mell, and nine-year-old daughter, Kate, in a midtown Manhattan flat, at 102 West 54th Street, around the corner from the Museum of Modern Art. Rothko did not like to work in neighborhoods where there were many other painters. Nor did he like to work at home where, he said, he felt he was under 'surveillance'. So his studio was located far downtown, at 222 Bowery, between Prince and Spring streets, in the old YMCA building; the cathedral-like space in which Rothko was painting had once been its gymnasium – its hardwood floor then (and, in 1991, still) covered with splotches of the blood-red paint Rothko was using in his murals. Painting for (or against) the rich, Rothko worked in a neighborhood of poverty, hunger, dereliction, homelessness. During the winter months, he would arrive at the studio wearing 'an old overcoat that came down to the ground' and 'a great big black hat that had a mouse hole eaten in the crown' – in short, looking more like a citizen of the Bowery than, say, a patron of the Four Seasons.

At fifty-six, Rothko, always a hefty bearlike man with a voracious appetite, had grown portly. Although he suffered from gout, he liked to each rich foods, he liked to drink, and he liked to smoke. His physician, Dr Albert Grokest, commented that Rothko's 'greatest sources of consolation were calories and alcohol'. Around this time, there were also signs of trouble in his marriage, with many arguments, and Mell Rothko, too, was developing a drinking problem.

With his paintings Rothko could create a place for himself. Within the last few years he had also made a place for himself in the world – an increasingly preeminent one. In late January of 1961, the Rothkos attended the inauguration of President John F. Kennedy. Getting Rothko into the proper clothes for such an occasion was, said one nephew, 'always an adventure'. Rothko rented the required tuxedo and, because of the alphabetical seating arrangement, was placed next to Walt Rostow, a member of the Kennedy 'brain trust' whom Rothko decided was 'mad'. Rothko himself, as one friend recalled, 'was riding high'.

Just three days before the inauguration, he had opened a two-month show at the Museum of Modern Art, becoming the first living member of his generation to have a one-man show at the museum. In the next two years, the exhibit would travel to London, Amsterdam, Basel, Rome, and Paris. Publicized by interview-articles in *Time* and *Newsweek* prior to the opening, the show received generally enthusiastic reviews, with one, by Robert Goldwater, providing what Rothko regarded as the most penetrating account ever written of his work. By 1960 Rothko's position in the art world and his financial position were secure enough so that he could, once he decided that the Four Seasons could not be transformed into the kind of 'place' he wished to create, return what he had been paid of his commission and withdraw the paintings.

For many years a kind of impoverished urban wanderer in New York, and still often dressing to look like one, Rothko, now receiving as much as $10,000 to $15,000 for his paintings, had just purchased his first home, a $75,000 four story painted brick house at 118 East 95th St., near Park Avenue. His wardrobe even improved – somewhat. 'Now that I have a bank account, I have a banker's coat', he joked. At fifty-eight Rothko was a proclaimed master and well-to-do. He had every reason to feel satisfied with himself.

Yet Rothko was a 'combative' person 'with an adversary view of human nature'. As an outsider, he had long felt bitter and deprived. Now as an insider he felt uneasy and contaminated. He had experienced 'anxiety about buying a house, becoming a property owner, no longer being poor'. To some of his friends, he complained that his wife and his accountant, Bernard Reis, had pressured him into buying the house. After all, if he was no longer poor, wronged, and marginal, then who was he? Moreover, a restless, lonely and gregarious person, Rothko had enjoyed hanging out in the bars and drugstores near his midtown 54th Street flat. Of his new neighborhood on New York's affluent Upper East Side, he complained that there were 'no friendly bars, no interesting jaunts or joints'. Success was producing its own headaches. 'He'd been fighting the world for so long,' said Anne-Marie Levine, 'he felt severely compromised by situations when the world paid him homage.'

Turning back the Seagram's commission reassured him that he had not compromised and was still the embattled outsider. Another consequence of success was the loss of friendships with some of the painters in his own generation to whom he had felt closest – men like Clyfford Still and Barnett Newman. 'There's no one to hang out with any more', he complained. 'They're too busy achieving things.' Younger painters, particularly the Pop artists, Rothko feared as eager to displace him: 'Those young artists are out to murder us', he warned. He may not have been entirely comfortable with the place he had made for himself in the world, but it had taken him so long to make it that he wasn't about to give it up.

The Museum of Modern Art show provided a crucial turning point. During the 1950s Rothko had lived in two flats, both of which were just a short walk from the museum: he spent many hours with its collection, he liked to hang out and hold forth in its coffee shop, and he often ran into Director Alfred Barr and Curator Dorothy Miller at the Valmor, a local Italian restaurant; 'he would often join us', Ms Miller recalled, and 'sit and talk for a while'. But he had long resented the museum's failure to give him the recognition he thought he deserved, when he had needed it most. The Modern 'has no convictions and no courage', he declared. 'It can't decide which paintings are good and which are bad. So it hedges by buying a little of everything.' Now he responded to the Museum's offer of a one-man exhibit with an angry grandiosity: 'They need me.

I don't need them. This show will lend dignity to the Museum. It does not lend dignity to me.'

Yet Rothko also felt a triumphant 'euphoria', as if the exhibit did confer position, even dignity. In fact, he was sufficiently aware of, and involved with, the museum's power to confer place in the art world to threaten withdrawing from the show if he couldn't get the particular floor in the museum he wanted. 'Of course, this was the biggest event in his life up to then', his friend Stanley Kunitz recalled, adding that Rothko behaved 'like a man obsessed during the whole period' before and during the exhibit. Originally scheduled for April–June 1960, the show had been twice put back on the museum's schedule; and Rothko had been planning the exhibit for at least eighteen months. Yet two days before the opening, he withdrew six works and added seven new ones to the exhibit. On the last day of the show, Rothko, who had tried to persuade the museum to extend it, 'was very reluctant for his show to end'. But, Kunitz added, Rothko also felt that his involvement 'was to a degree an act of self-betrayal because his caring so much about this show negated all that he'd been saying about the museum world'.

Regina Bogat, a young painter whose studio was across the hall, helped Rothko prepare for the exhibit. She recalled that 'his feeling about the Museum of Modern Art show was very intense. He became very busy and involved with his past, with his past work', and he had to take old paintings out of storage, unroll them, examine them and, for the ones he selected, he had to restore them, get them measured, and have stretchers made for them 'and it became a tremendous physical labor and time-consuming. He wondered what he was doing it for.' She finally asked why he was doing the show if it was causing him so much grief, and Rothko replied, 'I want to prove to my family that it was a good thing that I became a painter.' Both of Rothko's older brothers did attend the show, and one of them commented, after viewing fifty-seven of Rothko's works, 'I didn't know this place was so big.' So much for impressing the family.

After it opened, Rothko spent a great deal of time, almost daily, at the show. One young painter told him, 'Mark, it's a beautiful show' – to which Rothko replied. 'It's not a show, it's an event.' Yet Rothko hovered anxiously about, starting conversations with skeptical-looking strangers, trying to convert them. For all his grandiosity, Rothko himself was the doubter he was most struggling to convince. The January 16 opening was what newspapers call 'a gala event'. The invited guests included older artists from Albers to Hofmann, Davis to Duchamp, Dali to Hopper; it included all the living painters from Rothko's own generation (de Kooning and Kline, Motherwell and Newman), some younger painters such as Jasper Johns and Ray Parker, a few art critics (Clement Greenberg, Meyer Shapiro, Robert Goldwater), and more than a few dealers and collectors (Joseph Hirshorn and Paul Mellon). Rothko, who once said that 'when a crowd of people looks at a painting, I think of blasphemy', occupied the center of this profane rite.

'For all his gregariousness', writes John Hurt Fischer, remembering the opening, Rothko 'was shy; and since he was on display as much as his paintings, he began the evening in an agony of stage fright. Later, as one guest after another came to congratulate him – and usually to express an almost reverent admiration for his work – he relaxed and started to glow with affability.' After the black-tie reception at the museum, there were drinks at a bar on University Place. Then at five o'clock that morning, he showed up at a friend's apartment. 'I'm in despair', Rothko said. He was distraught, and he said, 'It's because everyone can see what a fraud I am.' With what he had chosen as the best of his life's work in front of him, his friends, and the public. Rothko felt exposed as worthless, empty. 'The whole enterprise was nothing', he declared, and Rothko's artistic enterprise *was*, after all, a something that was dangerously close to nothing. At the Museum of Modern Art opening, the moment of triumph he had worked so long and hard for had gone from stage fright through elation to humiliating despair.

Rothko's desire to create artistic works that would provide a place for him, his difficulty in accommodating these creations to the real world of restaurants, museums, and viewers, his combativeness, his prophetic ambitions, his intense desire for success, his guilt about success, his uncompromisingness, his compromises, his propensity to isolate himself, his wish for community, his mixed feelings about both wealth and poverty, his suspicions, his suspicions about himself, his vulnerability to despair – all these conflicting feelings in the Mark Rothko of the early 1960s had their origins in the life of Marcus Rothkowitz, born in Dvinsk, Russia, a despised Jew in the infamous Settlement of Pale, in the first years of the twentieth century.

E2 David Sylvester, 'Rothko'

From *New Statesman*, 20 October 1961, pp.36–7

Faced with Rothko's later paintings in the exhibition at Whitechapel, one feels oneself unbearably hemmed-in by forces buffeting one's every nerve, imagines the gravity of one's body to be multiplied as if some weight borne on one's shoulders were grinding one into the ground: one feels oneself rising against these pressures, riding them, carried away into exhilaration and release: pain and serenity become indistinguishable. This complex of feelings is familiar enough in the experience of tragic art, but tempered and complicated by other appeals to the senses and intellect and imagination – involvement in a specific type of human situation: the re-creation of familiar elements of reality in a way that makes them seem more real than in life: the benign equilibrium of a lucid architectonic structure: the poetic evocation of unexpected connections: the sensuous delight of beautiful colour or sound. There is nothing of all this in these paintings. Here emotion is unadulterated, isolated.

In retrospect, Rothko's image – a haunting image, I suspect, even for those who respond to its presence only mildly – provides its incidental satisfactions. It projects itself onto our vision of reality: looking along Park Avenue at the great glass-fronted slabs with their edges dissolving in the light, it is difficult not to be reminded of Rothko's looming, soft-edged stacks of rectangles. And it projects itself onto our taste: its combination of Indian red and brown and black can be rediscovered in fashionable ties and shirts of recent design.

But the evocative quality of the form, the seductive charm of the colour, become irrelevant when the paintings are confronted. These paintings are beyond poetry as they are beyond picture-making. To fantasise about them (as the catalogue does), discover storm-clouds or deserts in them, or sarcophagi, or aftermaths of nuclear explosions, is as corny as looking at Gothic architecture and thinking of the noonday twilight of the forest. These paintings begin and end with an intense and utterly direct expression of feeling through the interaction of coloured areas of a certain size. They are the complete fulfilment of Van Gogh's notion of using colour to convey man's passions. They are the realisation of what abstract artists have dreamed for 50 years of doing – making painting as inherently expressive as music. More than this: for not even with music, where the inevitable sense of the performer's activity introduces more of the effects of personality, does isolated emotion touch the nervous system so directly.

The claims which Rothko has made for his work seem on the surface decidedly perverse. He says he is 'no colourist', which might well be thought affected in view of the dully glowing splendour of his harmonies. He denies the view common among his admirers that his work is Apollonian, quietist, maintains that on the contrary it is nothing if not violent. Dionysian – the perverseness of this claim being that it seems pretty extravagant to attribute violent passion to paintings whose means of expression – the hushed colour, the design in terms of horizontals – are traditionally associated with serenity and stillness. But the claims are not perverse: it is not when he talks that Rothko is paradoxical but when he paints. The value of his painting lies precisely in the paradox that he uses seductive colour so that we disregard its seductiveness, that he uses the apparatus of serenity in achieving violence. For of course the stillness is there as well, and that is just the point: violence and serenity are reconciled and fused – this is what makes Rothko's a tragic art.

The achievement is parallel to Mondrian's who, using means the obvious potential of which was the creation of a perfectly static art, evolved a world of form in which stillness is locked with violent movement. Of this consummation in terms of the physical – to put it rather schematically –

Rothko's art is the equivalent in terms of the emotional. Their work is as it were the Parthenon and the Chartres of abstract painting – a vulgar analogy, perhaps, but one whose relevant implications include the point that a Mondrian dominates us as a compact entity out there, beyond our reach, a Rothko incorporates us, envelops us in its light. The analogy also serves to emphasise that a Rothko is awe-inspiring as a cathedral is, not as a mountain is: the effect of its scale is not to make us feel puny beside a sublime vastness. It has a scale transcendent enough to command, accessible enough to reassure.

The strength of the great monomaniacs of modern art – who also include Giacometti, Rosso, Monet – in relation to their audience is that they are not distracted by success or by failure. Their vulnerability is that they are peculiarly subject to hazards of presentation, since their work pushes the medium to extreme limits where there is no margin between glory and absurdity, so that, shown in the wrong light or at the wrong height, it can so easily go the other way. At Whitechapel the exhibition is worthy of the exhibits.

ACKNOWLEDGEMENTS

Grateful acknowledgement is made to the following sources for permission to reproduce material in this book:

King, M.L. Jr (1964) *Why We Can't Wait*, New American Library. Copyright © 1964 by Martin Luther King, Jr. Reprinted by permission of Joan Daves Agency; 'Letter from a young English academic', October 1963, courtesy of Professor Tony Tanner; Roszak, T. (1995) *The Making of a Counter Culture, Reflections on the Technocratic Society and Its Youthful Opposition*, University of California Press. © 1968, 1969 and 1995 by Theodore Roszak. Also by permission of International Creative Management, Inc.; Bluestone, H. and McGahee, C.L. (1962) 'Reaction to extreme stress: impending death by execution', *The American Journal of Psychiatry*, 119, November 1962, The American Psychiatric Association; Excerpt from *The Social Impact of Bomb Destruction*, by Fred Charles Ikle. Copyright © 1958 by the University of Oklahoma Press; Whitcomb, J.C. Jr and Morris, H.M. (1961) *The Genesis Flood: The Biblical Record and its Scientific Implications*, Baker, Grand Rapids, Michigan; Abstracted with permission from White, L. Jr (1967) 'The historical roots of our ecological crisis', *Science*, 155, No 3767, pp.1203–7. Copyright 1967 American Association for the Advancement of Science; Abstracted with permission from Hardin, G. (1968) 'The tragedy of the commons', *Science*, 162, No 3859, pp.1244–46 & 1248. Copyright 1968 American Association for the Advancement of Science; From *The Environmental Handbook* by Garrett De Bell. Copyright © 1970 by Garrett de Bell.